AI TODAY AND ITS EVOLUTION

ARAVIND

Clever Fox®
PUBLISHING

CLEVER FOX PUBLISHING
Chennai, India

Published by CLEVER FOX PUBLISHING 2025

Paperback ISBN: 978-93-7500-333-5
Hardback ISBN: 978-93-7500-912-2

PREFACE

Over the past decade, we've witnessed a breathtaking transformation in how machines learn, think, and even create. What was once confined to science fiction is now woven into the fabric of our daily lives, be it in how we shop, work, diagnose illness, or solve global problems. Writing this book has been a journey through the heart of that transformation, a way to capture not just the "what" of artificial intelligence, but also the "why" and "where next."

This book was born out of a personal passion for technology and a deep curiosity about its place in shaping our future. As I observed the growing influence of AI across industries, communities, and cultures, I realized the need to offer a clear and balanced guide that bridges the technical visionary and the practical user. My goal was to create something that speaks as naturally to the technologist as it does to the policy maker, the entrepreneur, or the everyday users trying to make sense of a fast-changing world with AI.

AI Today and Its Evolution is not just a book of information, it is a reflection of our shared future. It is a culmination of various research papers, articles, quantitative datapoints and real-world usage currently happening within AI world, powered by AI. Whether you are a student just stepping into the world of AI, a professional navigating its impacts, or a curious soul seeking understanding of AI world, this book is for you. May it inform you, inspire you, and perhaps most importantly, equip you to think critically and creatively in a world increasingly shaped by artificial intelligence.

INTRODUCTION

We are living through one of the most pivotal eras in human history. The rise of Artificial Intelligence isn't just another chapter in the evolution of technology, it's a turning point. AI is redefining industries, reshaping the economy, reimagining creativity, and challenging what it means to be human. And yet, for all its influence, AI remains misunderstood by many, wrapped in buzzwords, surrounded by hype, and shadowed by fear.

This book exists to cut through the noise. ***AI Today and Its Evolution*** invites you into a candid, grounded, and comprehensive exploration of AI. How it began, how it works, where it is now, and where it's heading. But more than that, it explores the heartbeat of this technology: its potential to empower, to disrupt, and to transform lives.

Across its chapters, this book will guide you from the foundations of machine learning and neural networks to the real-world applications in industries like healthcare, finance, real-estate, education, and sustainability. You'll explore ethical dilemmas, governance, and the philosophical questions AI provokes. You'll meet the promise and the peril head-on.

You don't have to be an expert to read this book. It's designed for thinkers, doers, and learners from all walks of life. Whether you're fascinated, sceptical, or simply curious, the pages ahead are meant to deepen your understanding and widen your perspective in the world of AI.

AI isn't just a tool. It's a mirror, a catalyst, and possibly the most powerful force we've ever created. So, let's explore it together, with open minds, sharp questions, and an eye toward the future.

CONTENTS

WHAT IS AI?
A HISTORY AND DEFINITION

1950–1960

THE BIRTH OF A DISCIPLINE

Dartmouth workshop in 1966 marked as academic field

- Symbolic AI
- Logic Theorist
- ELIZA

1970s–1980s

THE FIRST SETBACKS

Funding cuts

- Greater data availability
- Deep Blue vs. Garry Kasparov

2010s–Present

THE RISE OF AI

Increased computational power

- Big Data
- Algorithmic advancements
- ImageNet Challenge
- ChatGPT-4o

2010s-Present

CURRENT DEFINITION

Artificial intelligence: capability of a machine to imitate or surspass human intelligence.

CHAPTER 1

WHAT IS AI, ITS HISTORY AND CURRENT DEFINITION

The term "artificial intelligence" (AI) was first coined in 1956 at a workshop held at Dartmouth College, organized by John McCarthy. This event is widely considered the birth of AI as an academic discipline. However, the conceptual roots of AI stretch back much further, with philosophers and mathematicians pondering the nature of intelligence and the possibility of creating intelligent machines for centuries.

Early inspirations for AI can be found in ancient myths and legends featuring artificial beings, such as the bronze giant Talos in Greek mythology or the Golem of Jewish folklore. More concretely, the 17th century saw the development of mechanical calculators by figures like Blaise Pascal and Gottfried Wilhelm Leibniz, laying some of the groundwork for automated computation.

The 19th century brought the analytical engine conceived by Charles Babbage and further developed by Ada Lovelace, who is often credited with writing the first algorithm intended to be carried out by a machine. Although mechanical, these inventions introduced the idea of programmable machines capable of performing complex tasks.

The true intellectual foundations for modern AI were laid in the first half of the 20th century. Pioneering work in mathematical logic and computation by figures like Alan Turing and Alonzo Church was crucial. Alan Turing, in particular, is often regarded as the father of AI. His 1950 paper, "Computing Machinery and Intelligence," introduced the "Turing Test" as a criterion for machine intelligence and explored the possibility of machines thinking. This paper provided a foundational concept for the field, shifting the focus from simply building machines that could calculate to building machines that could reason and learn.

The Birth of a Discipline (1950s-1960s)

The Dartmouth workshop in 1956 marked the formal beginning of AI research. Key figures like John McCarthy, Marvin Minsky, Nathaniel Rochester, and Claude Shannon gathered to explore how machines could simulate aspects of human intelligence. This period was characterized by immense optimism and groundbreaking work in symbolic AI, focusing on problem-solving through logical reasoning and search algorithms.

Early AI programs included the Logic Theorist (1956) by Allen Newell, Herbert A. Simon, and J.C. Shaw, which could prove mathematical theorems, and ELIZA (1966) by Joseph Weizenbaum, a natural language processing program that simulated a Rogerian psychotherapist. These early successes fueled the belief that human-level AI was just around the corner.

The AI Winters (1970s-1980s)

Despite initial enthusiasm, the limitations of early AI approaches became apparent. Programs often struggled with real-world complexity, common sense reasoning, and scaling beyond narrow, well-defined problems. Funding for AI research dwindled, leading to the first "AI winter" in the mid-1970s. The Lighthill Report in the UK (1973) was particularly influential in cutting government funding for AI research due to its pessimistic assessment of the field's progress.

The 1980s saw a resurgence of interest, largely driven by the rise of expert systems. These AI programs encoded human expert knowledge to solve complex problems in specific domains, such as medical diagnosis (MYCIN) or configuring computer systems (R1/XCON). Japan's ambitious Fifth Generation Computer Systems project also spurred global interest and investment in AI. However, the limitations of expert systems (e.g., difficulty in knowledge acquisition, brittleness outside their narrow domains) eventually led to another downturn, the second AI winter, by the late 1980s.

The Resurgence and Machine Learning Era (1990s-2000s)

During the AI winters, research continued, often under different names like "machine learning" or "data mining." This period saw a shift from symbolic AI to more statistical and data-driven approaches. Key developments included:

- **Machine Learning:** Algorithms like support vector machines (SVMs) and decision trees gained prominence. These methods focused on enabling computers to learn from data without explicit programming, a significant departure from earlier rule-based systems.
- **Data Availability:** The rise of the internet and digital data collection provided the fuel for these data-driven approaches. Large datasets became increasingly available, allowing machine learning models to be trained on real-world information.
- **Deep Blue vs. Garry Kasparov (1997):** IBM's Deep Blue chess program defeated world champion Garry Kasparov, a landmark event that captured public imagination and demonstrated AI's growing capabilities in complex strategic games.

The Deep Learning Revolution (2010s-Present)

The 2010s witnessed an explosive growth in AI, largely driven by the deep learning revolution. This was facilitated by several factors:

- **Increased Computational Power:** The advent of powerful Graphics Processing Units (GPUs), originally designed for video games, proved to be highly effective for the parallel computations required by neural networks.
- **Big Data:** The exponential growth of digital data, from social media to scientific instruments, provided unprecedented amounts of training data for deep learning models.
- **Algorithmic Advancements:** Innovations in neural network architectures, such as convolutional neural networks (CNNs) for image processing and recurrent neural networks (RNNs)

for sequential data, significantly improved performance in tasks like image recognition and natural language processing.

Landmark achievements during this period include:

- **ImageNet Challenge (2012):** AlexNet, a deep convolutional neural network, significantly outperformed traditional methods in the ImageNet Large Scale Visual Recognition Challenge, marking a turning point for deep learning in computer vision.
- **AlphaGo (2016):** DeepMind's AlphaGo defeated the world champion Go player, Lee Sedol, a feat previously thought to be decades away due to the immense complexity of the game.
- **Transformer Architecture (2017):** The introduction of the Transformer architecture revolutionized natural language processing, leading to the development of highly powerful language models like BERT, GPT-2, and GPT-3. This architecture enabled models to process long sequences of text more efficiently and effectively.

The AI Boom and Generative AI (2020s)

The 2020s have been characterized by an unprecedented "AI boom," primarily driven by the widespread availability and capabilities of generative AI models. These models, built upon the Transformer architecture and trained on massive datasets, can generate highly realistic and coherent text, images, audio, and even video.

- **ChatGPT (2022):** OpenAI's release of ChatGPT brought generative AI into mainstream public consciousness, showcasing its ability to engage in human-like conversation, write code, compose essays, and much more. This sparked a wave of interest and investment in large language models (LLMs).

- **Diffusion Models:** Advancements in diffusion models have led to impressive text-to-image generation capabilities (e.g., DALL-E, Midjourney, Stable Diffusion), allowing users to create complex and artistic images from simple text prompts.

This period of rapid progress has also intensified discussions around the ethical implications of AI, including concerns about misinformation, copyright, job displacement, and the need for robust AI governance and regulation.

Current Definition of AI

Defining Artificial Intelligence precisely remains a complex and evolving task, as the field is constantly pushing the boundaries of what machines can achieve. However, a widely accepted contemporary definition views AI as **the ability of a machine or computer system to perform tasks that typically require human intelligence.** This definition is broad, encompassing a spectrum of capabilities and approaches, and it highlights the aspirational nature of the field – to create machines that can mimic, and in some cases surpass, human cognitive functions.

To elaborate, this definition implies several key aspects:

- **Cognitive Simulation:** AI aims to simulate various cognitive functions associated with the human mind. These include:
  - **Learning:** The ability to acquire knowledge and skills through experience, data, and observation, and to improve performance over time without explicit programming. This

is the cornerstone of modern AI, particularly in machine learning and deep learning.

- **Reasoning:** The capacity to apply logic, rules, and inferences to draw conclusions, solve problems, and make decisions. This involves both deductive reasoning (from general principles to specific conclusions) and inductive reasoning (from specific observations to general principles).
- **Problem-Solving:** The capability to identify problems, analyze their components, and devise strategies to find optimal or satisfactory solutions. This can range from simple puzzles to complex real-world challenges.
- **Perception:** The interpretation and understanding of sensory information from the environment. This includes computer vision (interpreting images and videos), speech recognition (understanding spoken language), and other forms of sensory data processing.
- **Natural Language Understanding and Generation (NLU/NLG):** The ability to comprehend, interpret, and generate human language in both written and spoken forms. This allows AI systems to communicate with humans naturally and to process vast amounts of textual information.
- **Decision-Making:** The process of making choices or selecting actions based on available information, predefined objectives, and learned patterns. This often involves evaluating probabilities and potential outcomes.
- **Creativity:** While traditionally considered a uniquely human trait, AI is increasingly demonstrating creative capabilities, such as generating original art, music, text, and even designing new molecules or architectural plans. This

involves combining existing knowledge in novel ways to produce something new and valuable.

- **Adaptability and Autonomy:** Modern AI systems are designed to be adaptive, meaning they can adjust their behavior and improve their performance based on new data and experiences. They also exhibit varying degrees of autonomy, operating independently to achieve their goals once deployed.
- **Broad Range of Techniques:** The field of AI is not monolithic; it encompasses a diverse array of techniques and subfields. These include:
    - **Machine Learning (ML):** A core subset of AI that focuses on algorithms enabling systems to learn from data. This includes supervised learning, unsupervised learning, and reinforcement learning.
    - **Deep Learning (DL):** A specialized branch of machine learning that uses artificial neural networks with multiple layers (deep neural networks) to learn complex patterns from large datasets, leading to breakthroughs in areas like image and speech recognition.
    - **Natural Language Processing (NLP):** The area of AI concerned with the interaction between computers and human language.
    - **Computer Vision:** Enables computers to interpret and understand visual information from the world, such as images and videos, allowing them to 'see' and make sense of their surroundings.

Conclusion

Ultimately the goal is for Artificial General Intelligence (AGI), a hypothetical AI that can understand, learn, and apply intelligence to any intellectual task that a human being can. In essence, AI has evolved from a theoretical concept to a transformative technology that is continually pushing the boundaries of what machines can achieve. While the aspiration of Artificial General Intelligence (AGI) remains a long-term goal, the current capabilities of specialized AI systems are already reshaping industries and daily life. This foundational understanding of AI's past, present, and core definitions sets the stage for exploring its diverse applications and future implications in the subsequent chapters of this book.

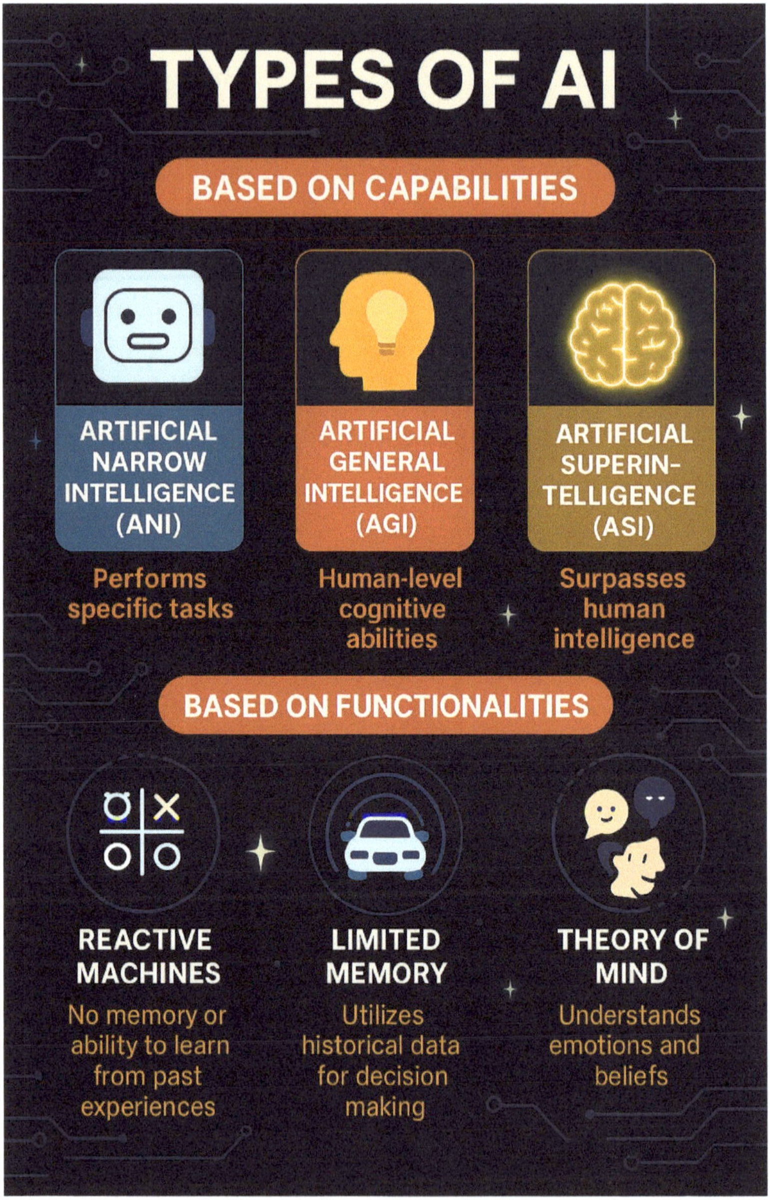
TYPES OF AI
BASED ON CAPABILITIES
ARTIFICIAL NARROW INTELLIGENCE (ANI)
Performs specific tasks
ARTIFICIAL GENERAL INTELLIGENCE (AGI)
Human-level cognitive abilities
ARTIFICIAL SUPERIN-TELLIGENCE (ASI)
Surpasses human intelligence
BASED ON FUNCTIONALITIES
REACTIVE MACHINES
No memory or ability to learn from past experiences
LIMITED MEMORY
Utilizes historical data for decision making
THEORY OF MIND
Understands emotions and beliefs

CHAPTER 2

WHAT ARE THE TYPES OF AI TODAY

Artificial intelligence can be categorized in several ways, often based on its capabilities and functionalities. Understanding these distinctions is essential for understanding the current landscape of AI and its potential future.

Types of AI Based on Capabilities

AI systems are often classified into three types based on their capacity to mimic human intelligence:

1. Artificial Narrow Intelligence (ANI) / Weak AI

Artificial Narrow Intelligence, also known as Weak AI, is the only type of AI that currently exists. ANI systems are designed and trained for a specific task. They can perform their designated task exceptionally well, often surpassing human capabilities in speed and efficiency. However, their intelligence is limited to their programmed function, and they cannot perform tasks outside of their defined scope or transfer knowledge to different domains.

Real-world Use Cases:

- **Virtual Personal Assistants:** Siri, Alexa, and Google Assistant are prime examples of ANI. They excel at understanding and responding to voice commands, setting alarms, playing music, and providing information, but their intelligence is confined to these specific functions.
- **Recommendation Systems:** Platforms like Netflix, Amazon, and YouTube use ANI to analyze user behavior and preferences to suggest movies, products, or videos. These systems are highly effective within their domain but cannot perform other intelligent tasks.

2. Artificial General Intelligence (AGI) / Strong AI

Artificial General Intelligence, or Strong AI, is a theoretical concept. AGI would possess the ability to understand, learn, and apply intelligence to any intellectual task that a human being can. An AGI system would be capable of learning new skills, solving unfamiliar problems, adapting to varied situations without explicit programming. It would have cognitive abilities comparable to a human.

Real-world Use Cases (Theoretical):

- **Advanced Scientific Research:** An AGI could potentially accelerate scientific discovery by independently formulating hypotheses, designing experiments, analyzing complex data, and drawing conclusions across multiple scientific disciplines.
- **Universal Problem Solver:** Imagine an AGI capable of solving any complex global issue, from climate change to disease

eradication, by integrating knowledge from diverse fields and devising innovative solutions.

3. Artificial Superintelligence (ASI)

Artificial Superintelligence is also a theoretical concept, representing an AI that would not only match but surpass human intelligence in virtually every field, including creativity, general wisdom, and problem-solving. ASI would be capable of cognitive abilities far beyond what humans can achieve.

Real-world Use Cases (Theoretical):

- **Global Optimization and Management:** An ASI could manage and optimize global resources, logistics, and systems with unparalleled efficiency, leading to solutions for complex societal challenges like poverty, resource scarcity, and environmental degradation.
- **Rapid Technological Advancement:** An ASI could drive technological progress at an exponential rate, leading to breakthroughs in science, engineering, and medicine that are currently unimaginable.

Types of AI Based on Functionalities

Within the realm of Artificial Narrow Intelligence, AI systems can be further categorized based on their functional capabilities:

1. Reactive Machines

Reactive machines are the most basic type of AI. They have no memory and cannot use past experiences to inform future decisions. They simply react to current situations based on their programming. They operate on a set of predefined rules and are designed to perform specific, repetitive tasks.

Real-world Use Cases:

- **IBM Deep Blue:** The chess-playing supercomputer that defeated Garry Kasparov in the 1990s is a classic example. Deep Blue could analyze the current state of the chessboard and predict optimal moves, but it had no memory of past games or the ability to learn from them.
- **Spam Filters:** Many early spam filters are reactive machines. They identify and filter out emails based on predefined patterns and keywords, without learning from past interactions or adapting to new spamming techniques.

2. Limited Memory AI

Limited Memory AI systems can look into the past to make decisions. They can store and use past data for a short period to make predictions or take actions. This type of AI is more complex than reactive machines and forms the basis for most of the AI applications we use today.

Real-world Use Cases:

- **Self-Driving Cars:** Autonomous vehicles use limited memory AI to observe their surroundings (e.g., speed of nearby cars, lane markings, traffic lights) and combine this with recent historical data (e.g., trajectory of other vehicles) to make immediate driving decisions.
- **Generative AI (e.g., ChatGPT, Bard now Gemini):** These models use limited memory to generate coherent and contextually relevant text. They consider the preceding words and sentences in a conversation to predict and produce the next most probable sequence of words, creating a fluid dialogue.

3. Theory of Mind AI (Theoretical)

Theory of Mind AI is a theoretical concept that refers to AI systems capable of understanding emotions, beliefs, intentions, and desires of other intelligent entities (humans or other AI). This level of AI would be able to infer human motives and reasoning, leading to more nuanced and personalized interactions.

Real-world Use Cases (Theoretical):

- **Empathetic Virtual Companions:** Imagine AI companions that can genuinely understand and respond to human emotions, providing personalized support and companionship based on a deep comprehension of the user's mental state.
- **Advanced Negotiation Agents:** AI systems capable of understanding the motivations and emotional states of human negotiators, allowing them to adapt their strategies for more effective and mutually beneficial outcomes.

4. Self-Aware AI (Theoretical)

Self-Aware AI is the most advanced and purely theoretical type of AI. It would possess consciousness, self-awareness, and its own beliefs, desires, and emotions. This level of AI would be able to understand its own internal states and traits, as well as those of others.

Real-world Use Cases (Theoretical):

- **Autonomous Research and Development:** A self-aware AI could independently pursue scientific research, driven by its own curiosity and understanding, leading to unprecedented breakthroughs across all fields of knowledge.
- **Ethical Decision-Making Systems:** A self-aware AI, with its own understanding of morality and ethics, could potentially make complex ethical decisions in critical situations, such as resource allocation in a crisis, with a profound understanding of the implications.

Emerging AI Categories and Their Applications

Beyond the traditional classifications, several new categories of AI are gaining prominence, each with distinct capabilities and real-world impact:

1. Predictive AI

Predictive AI focuses on forecasting future outcomes or behaviors based on historical data and statistical models. It identifies patterns and relationships within data to make informed predictions, enabling proactive decision-making.

Real-world Use Cases:

- **Demand Forecasting in Retail:** Retailers use predictive AI to analyze past sales data, seasonality, promotions, and external factors (like weather) to accurately forecast future product demand. This optimizes inventory levels, reduces waste, and prevents stockouts.
- **Predictive Maintenance in Manufacturing:** In industrial settings, predictive AI monitors sensor data from machinery to anticipate equipment failures before they occur. This allows for scheduled maintenance, minimizing downtime, reducing repair costs, and extending the lifespan of assets.

2. Conversational AI

Conversational AI enables machines to understand, process, and respond to human language in a natural and intuitive way. It encompasses technologies like natural language processing (NLP), machine learning, and speech recognition to facilitate human-like conversations.

Real-world Use Cases:

- **Customer Service Chatbots and Virtual Assistants:** Many businesses deploy conversational AI in the form of chatbots on websites or virtual assistants in call centers to handle customer inquiries, provide support, and automate routine tasks. This improves response times and frees up human agents for more complex issues.

- **Voice Assistants (e.g., Google Assistant, Alexa, Siri):** These widely used applications allow users to interact with devices and access information using voice commands. Conversational AI enables them to understand diverse accents, intentions, and contexts to provide relevant responses or perform requested actions.

3. Generative AI

Generative AI refers to AI systems capable of creating new, original content, such as text, images, audio, video, and even code, that resembles human-created output. These models learn patterns and structures from existing data to generate novel outputs.

Real-world Use Cases:

- **Content Creation (Text and Images):** Generative AI models like GPT-3/GPT-4 (for text) and DALL-E/Midjourney (for images) are used to generate articles, marketing copy, creative stories, and realistic or artistic images. This accelerates content production for various industries, from marketing to entertainment.
- **Drug Discovery and Material Design:** In scientific research, generative AI can design novel molecules or materials with desired properties. By exploring vast chemical spaces, these models can propose new compounds for drug development or materials with specific functionalities, significantly speeding up innovation.

4. Agentic AI

Agentic AI refers to AI systems designed to act autonomously to achieve specific goals, often by breaking down complex tasks into smaller sub-tasks, executing them, and reflecting on the results. These agents can plan, execute, and self-correct their actions in dynamic environments.

Real-world Use Cases:

- **Autonomous Robotics and Drones:** Agentic AI powers robots and drones that can navigate complex environments, perform tasks (e.g., inspection, delivery), and adapt to unforeseen circumstances without constant human intervention. This is crucial in fields like logistics, agriculture, and exploration.
- **Automated Software Development and Testing:** Agentic AI systems can generate code, identify bugs, and even write and execute test cases autonomously. This streamlines the software development lifecycle, improving efficiency and reducing human error in coding and quality assurance.

Key AI Technologies and Concepts

Beyond these classifications, several core technologies and concepts underpin the development and application of AI:

Machine Learning (ML)

Machine Learning is a subset of AI that enables systems to learn from data without being explicitly programmed. It involves algorithms that build a model from sample data, known as "training data," to make predictions or decisions. ML is foundational to most modern AI applications.

Real-world Use Cases:

- **Fraud Detection:** Financial institutions use ML algorithms to analyze transaction patterns and identify anomalies that may indicate fraudulent activity, learning from past instances of fraud to improve detection rates.
- **Medical Diagnosis:** ML models are trained on vast datasets of patient information, including symptoms, medical history, and test results, to assist doctors in diagnosing diseases with higher accuracy.

Deep Learning (DL)

Deep Learning is a subfield of machine learning that uses artificial neural networks with multiple layers (hence "deep") to learn from vast amounts of data. DL has been particularly successful in tasks involving complex patterns, such as image and speech recognition.

Real-world Use Cases:

- **Image Recognition:** Deep learning powers facial recognition systems, object detection in autonomous vehicles, and image classification in various applications by learning intricate features from pixel data.
- **Speech Recognition:** Virtual assistants and transcription services rely on deep learning to accurately convert spoken

language into text, understanding different accents, tones, and speech patterns.

Natural Language Processing (NLP)

Natural Language Processing is an AI field focused on enabling computers to understand, interpret, and generate human language. NLP combines computational linguistics, machine learning, and deep learning to process and analyze large amounts of natural language data.

Real-world Use Cases:

- **Sentiment Analysis:** Businesses use NLP to analyze customer reviews, social media posts, and feedback to gauge public opinion about products or services, identifying positive, negative, or neutral sentiments.
- **Machine Translation:** Services like Google Translate use NLP to translate text or speech from one language to another, facilitating global communication.

Computer Vision (CV)

Computer Vision is an AI field that trains computers to "see" and interpret the visual world. It enables machines to process, analyze, and understand images and videos, mimicking human visual perception.

Real-world Use Cases:

- **Quality Control in Manufacturing:** CV systems inspect products on assembly lines for defects, ensuring quality and consistency by identifying deviations from predefined standards.
- **Security and Surveillance:** CV is used in surveillance systems for facial recognition, anomaly detection, and tracking objects or individuals in real-time.

Robotics

Robotics is an interdisciplinary field that integrates AI with engineering to design, build, operate, and apply robots. AI enables robots to perceive their environment, make decisions, and perform tasks autonomously or semi-autonomously.

Real-world Use Cases:

- **Industrial Automation:** Robots with AI capabilities are widely used in manufacturing for tasks like assembly, welding, and material handling, improving efficiency and precision.
- **Surgical Robots:** AI-powered robots assist surgeons in performing complex procedures with greater accuracy and minimal invasiveness, enhancing patient outcomes.

Expert Systems and Knowledge-Based Systems

Expert systems are early forms of AI that use a knowledge base of human expertise to solve problems that typically require human intelligence. They are designed to mimic the decision-making ability of a human expert within a specific domain.

Real-world Use Cases:

- **Medical Diagnosis Systems:** Early expert systems were developed to assist doctors in diagnosing diseases by asking a series of questions and applying rules based on medical knowledge.
- **Financial Planning:** Some financial advisory systems use expert system principles to provide personalized investment advice based on a client's financial situation and goals.

These diverse types and technologies of AI highlight the breadth and depth of its current applications and the theoretical possibilities that continue to drive research and innovation in the field. As AI continues to evolve, the lines between these categories may blur, and new forms of intelligence may emerge, further transforming our world.

Conclusion

To summarize, artificial intelligence isn't just one thing, it's a vast landscape of ideas, systems, and technologies evolving at an extraordinary pace. From simple tools that react to input, to more advanced systems capable of learning, predicting, and even generating new ideas, AI is becoming more integrated into our everyday lives.

This journey through the different forms and functions of AI shows us that we're standing at a unique moment in technological history. We're no longer just imagining what machines can do, we're living it. What makes this especially exciting is how these innovations are not only solving problems but also opening new possibilities in how we live, work, and think.

Understanding these layers of AI helps us make sense of where we are and where we might be headed. It prepares us to ask the right questions, make better decisions, and be actively involved in shaping how AI continues to develop for the greater good. The future isn't written yet, but with the right awareness and intention, we can guide AI to serve us all in meaningful, human-centered ways.

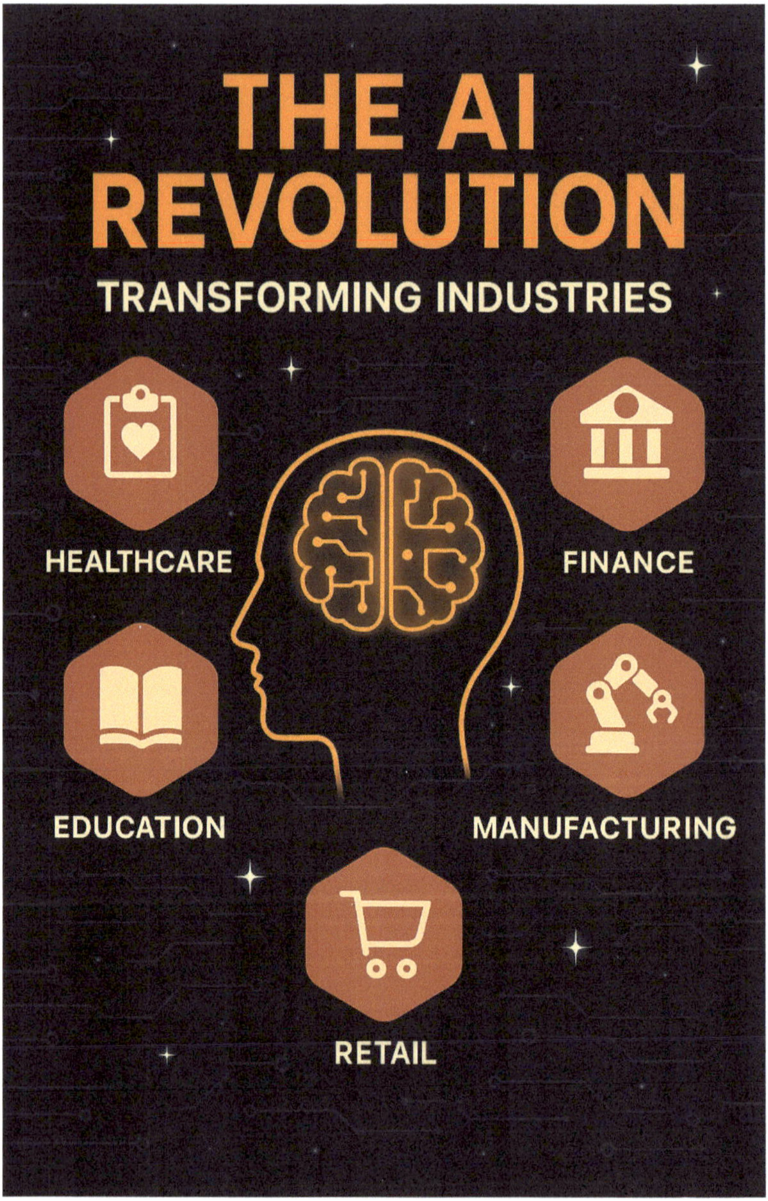
THE AI
REVOLUTION
TRANSFORMING INDUSTRIES
HEALTHCARE
FINANCE
EDUCATION
MANUFACTURING
RETAIL

CHAPTER 3

THE AI REVOLUTION: TRANSFORMING INDUSTRIES AND HUMANITY

Artificial intelligence is not merely a technological advancement; it is a profound revolution reshaping societies, economies, and the very fabric of human interaction. Its impact is far-reaching, driving unprecedented changes across diverse industries and fundamentally altering the way we live, work, and create. This chapter delves into the transformative power of AI, with a particular emphasis on its influence on the technology industry, supported by quantitative data and an analysis of its broader benefits.

AI's Broad Impact on Humanity

The AI revolution is changing humanity in profound and multifaceted ways, from enhancing daily life to posing complex ethical questions. On a societal level, AI is contributing to advancements in healthcare, education, and accessibility, while also raising concerns about job displacement, privacy, and algorithmic bias.

AI in Healthcare: A Revolution in Well-being

AI is deeply transforming healthcare, moving towards a more predictive, preventive, personalized, and participatory (P4) model of medicine. Its applications are directly impacting individuals' health outcomes and the efficiency of healthcare systems.

- **Enhanced Diagnostics and Disease Detection:** AI algorithms can analyze medical images (X-rays, MRIs, CT scans), pathology slides, and genomic data with remarkable speed and accuracy, often surpassing human capabilities in detecting subtle anomalies. For instance, AI-powered systems can detect early signs of diseases like cancer, diabetic retinopathy, and cardiovascular conditions, leading to earlier interventions and improved prognoses. This means individuals can receive diagnoses faster and more accurately, potentially saving lives and reducing the burden of advanced disease.
- **Personalized Treatment Plans:** AI enables the creation of highly personalized treatment regimens by analyzing a patient's unique genetic makeup, medical history, lifestyle, and response to previous treatments. This precision medicine approach ensures that individuals receive therapies most likely to be effective for them, minimizing trial-and-error and improving treatment efficacy. For example, in oncology, AI can help identify the most suitable chemotherapy or immunotherapy based on a tumor's genetic profile.
- **Drug Discovery and Development:** The process of discovering new drugs is notoriously long, expensive, and prone to failure. AI accelerates this by rapidly screening vast libraries of compounds, predicting molecular interactions, and identifying

potential drug candidates. This significantly reduces the time and cost associated with bringing new life-saving medications to market, benefiting patients globally.

- **Remote Monitoring and Predictive Health:** Wearable devices and AI-powered remote monitoring systems allow individuals to track their health metrics (heart rate, sleep patterns, activity levels) continuously. AI analyzes this data to identify deviations from baseline, predict potential health issues before they become critical, and provide personalized health recommendations. This empowers individuals to take a more proactive role in managing their health and can prevent hospitalizations.
- **Streamlined Administrative Tasks:** AI automates routine administrative tasks in healthcare, such as patient scheduling, billing, electronic health record management, and insurance claims processing. This frees up healthcare professionals to dedicate more time to direct patient care, improving the overall patient experience and reducing operational costs.

AI in Education: Tailoring Learning for Every Student

AI is revolutionizing education by making learning more personalized, accessible, and engaging, adapting to the unique needs and pace of individual learners.

- **Personalized Learning Pathways:** AI-powered adaptive learning platforms assess a student strength, weaknesses, and learning style, then tailor content, exercises, and teaching methods accordingly. This ensures that each student receives instruction at their optimal level, leading to improved comprehension and retention. For example, AI tutors can provide immediate feedback and guide students through challenging concepts step-by-step.

- **Intelligent Tutoring Systems:** AI tutors offer personalized, on-demand support, mimicking the interaction with a human tutor. They can answer questions, provide explanations, suggest practice problems, and identify areas where a student needs additional help. This supplementary support can significantly enhance learning outcomes, especially for students who may not have access to one-on-one human tutoring.
- **Automated Assessment and Feedback:** AI can automate the grading of assignments, essays, and exams, providing instant feedback to students. This not only reduces the workload for educators but also allows students to learn from their mistakes more quickly and effectively. AI can also identify common misconceptions across a class, enabling teachers to adjust their instruction.
- **Accessibility for Diverse Learners:** AI tools are breaking down barriers for students with disabilities. Text-to-speech and speech-to-text technologies, real-time translation, and AI-powered captioning make educational content accessible to students with visual or hearing impairments, language barriers, or learning disabilities. This fosters a more inclusive learning environment.
- **Administrative Efficiency for Educators:** AI automates routine administrative tasks for teachers, such as managing student records, scheduling, and generating reports. This frees up valuable time, allowing educators to focus more on teaching,

curriculum development, and building stronger relationships with their students.

AI and Overall Productivity: Amplifying Human Potential

AI is a powerful catalyst for boosting productivity at both individual and organizational levels, automating mundane tasks and augmenting human capabilities across various domains.

- **Automation of Repetitive Tasks:** AI excels at automating routine, rule-based, and high-volume tasks that traditionally consume significant human time. This includes data entry, scheduling, email management, report generation, and customer service inquiries. By offloading these tasks to AI, individuals can redirect their energy to more complex, creative, and strategic work, leading to substantial productivity gains.
- **Intelligent Assistants and Workflow Optimization:** AI-powered virtual assistants and smart software tools help individuals manage their schedules, prioritize tasks, and streamline workflows. They can analyze user habits, suggest optimal times for tasks, and integrate with various applications to create seamless work environments. This leads to better time management and reduced cognitive load.
- **Enhanced Decision-Making:** AI processes and analyzes vast amounts of data much faster and more comprehensively than humans, identifying patterns and insights that inform better decision-making. This is crucial in complex environments where human cognitive limitations might lead to suboptimal choices.

- **Content Creation and Communication:** Generative AI tools assist in drafting emails, summarizing documents, creating presentations, and even generating creative content like marketing copy or design ideas. This significantly accelerates content creation processes, allowing individuals to produce high-quality output more efficiently.
- **Personalized Information Management:** AI helps individuals manage the overwhelming influx of information by filtering, summarizing, and prioritizing content based on their interests and needs. This ensures that individuals focus on the most relevant information, enhancing their learning and decision-making processes.
- **Skill Augmentation and Learning:** AI tools can act as personal coaches or learning companions, providing tailored feedback and resources to help individuals acquire new skills or improve existing ones. This continuous learning capability directly contributes to individual growth and adaptability in a rapidly changing world.

AI's Transformative Influence Across Industries

AI's impact is felt across nearly every industry, driving efficiency, innovation, and new business models. From optimizing supply chains to revolutionizing customer service, AI is a key driver of economic growth and competitive advantage.

- **Healthcare:** As discussed in Chapter 2, AI is transforming healthcare through improved diagnostics, accelerated drug discovery, and personalized medicine. The global AI in healthcare market size was valued at **USD 500 billion by 2032** and is projected to grow significantly, indicating the massive investment and adoption in this sector.

- **Finance:** AI enhances fraud detection, algorithmic trading, and risk management. AI-powered systems can analyze millions of transactions in real-time, identifying fraudulent activities with high accuracy. This has led to substantial savings for financial institutions. For example, AI-driven fraud detection systems can reduce false positives by **up to 50%**, saving banks millions of dollars annually.
- **Transportation:** Autonomous vehicles, intelligent traffic management systems, and optimized logistics are revolutionizing transportation. AI-powered traffic management systems can reduce urban congestion by **10-25%**, leading to reduced travel times and fuel consumption.
- **Education:** AI is personalizing learning experiences, automating administrative tasks, and providing intelligent tutoring. Adaptive learning platforms, powered by AI, can improve student engagement and learning outcomes by **up to 20%** by tailoring content to individual needs.
- **Manufacturing:** AI is driving predictive maintenance, quality control, and robotic automation in manufacturing. Predictive maintenance, enabled by AI, can reduce equipment downtime by **20-50%** and increase asset lifespan by **20-40%**, leading to significant cost savings.
- **Retail and E-commerce:** AI-driven recommendation engines, customer service chatbots, and inventory optimization are reshaping retail. Recommendation engines, for instance, are responsible for **up to 35% of Amazon's revenue**, demonstrating their direct impact on sales.

Emphasis on the Technology Industry

The technology industry itself is at the forefront of the AI revolution, with software developers steadily becoming one of the biggest beneficiaries of the AI advancement. AI is fundamentally changing how software is developed, how data is managed, and how technological products and services are delivered.

Software Development and Engineering: The Rise of Vibe Coding and Vibe Flows

AI is increasingly being used to automate various stages of the software development lifecycle. AI-powered tools assist with code generation, bug detection, and automated testing. This has given rise to concepts like **"vibe coding"** and **"vibe flows."**

Vibe coding refers to an approach where developers heavily rely on large language models (LLMs) to generate code. Instead of writing code line by line, developers describe their intentions or desired functionality in natural language, and the AI translates these ideas into executable code. This paradigm shifts the developers role from a hands-on coder to a more strategic architect and editor, focusing on guiding the AI, reviewing its output, and ensuring the generated code aligns with project requirements and best practices.

This approach fosters **vibe flows**, which describe the state of continuous, intuitive, and highly productive workflow enabled by AI integration. By offloading repetitive, boilerplate, or complex coding tasks to AI, developers can maintain a deeper focus on problem-solving, innovation, and the overall system design.

The AI acts as an intelligent assistant, anticipating needs, suggesting solutions, and rapidly generating code snippets, allowing developers to stay in a creative "flow state" without being bogged down by syntax or routine implementation details.

Quantitative Impact:

- **Increased Developer Productivity:** Studies and early adoption indicate significant boosts in developer productivity. For instance, tools like GitHub Copilot have been reported to help developer's complete tasks **up to 40% faster**. This acceleration is attributed to the AI's ability to quickly generate code, suggest relevant functions, and automate repetitive coding patterns.
- **Reduced Time-to-Market:** By streamlining the coding process and accelerating development cycles, vibe coding contributes to a faster time-to-market for new software products and features. This agility is crucial in today's rapidly evolving technological landscape.
- **Lowered Barrier to Entry:** Vibe coding can democratize software development by enabling individuals with strong logical thinking and problem-solving skills, but limited coding experience, to contribute effectively. This expands the talent pool and fosters innovation from diverse backgrounds.

Another term called **"vibe stack"** refers to the collection of AI-powered tools and platforms that facilitate vibe coding and enable these enhanced development workflows. Some prominent examples include:

- **GitHub Copilot:** A leading AI pair programmer developed by GitHub and OpenAI. It provides real-time code suggestions, autocompletions, and even entire function bodies based on comments and existing code. It supports numerous programming languages and integrates seamlessly with popular Integrated Development Environment or IDE.

- **Vercel v0:** This platform exemplifies generative UI. Developers can describe desired user interface components or even entire web pages using natural language, and v0 generates the corresponding code (e.g., React, HTML, CSS). This significantly accelerates frontend development and prototyping.
- **Cursor:** An AI-first code editor designed from the ground up to integrate LLMs into the coding experience. It allows developers to chat with their code, ask questions, generate new code, and debug using natural language prompts, making the development process more conversational and intuitive.
- **Replit AI:** Integrated into the Replit online IDE, Replit AI provides a suite of AI-powered features, including code completion, code generation, debugging assistance, and even the ability to transform natural language descriptions into functional code. It aims to provide a comprehensive AI-augmented development environment.
- **Bolt.new and Lovable:** These emerging platforms focus on rapid application development through AI. They often combine AI-driven code generation with visual development tools, allowing users to quickly build and deploy applications with minimal manual coding.

These tools are not just automating coding; they are fundamentally changing the developer experience, fostering a more intuitive, efficient, and creative approach to building software.

The rise of vibe coding and vibe flows signifies a new era where human ingenuity is amplified by intelligent AI assistants, pushing the boundaries of what's possible in the technology industry.

Other Impacts on the Technology Industry

- **Data Management and Analytics:** The explosion of data in the digital age has made AI indispensable for data management and analytics. AI algorithms can process, clean, and analyze massive datasets to extract valuable insights beyond human capability. This enables data-driven decision-making across all tech companies, from product development to marketing strategies. The global big data analytics market, heavily reliant on AI, is projected to reach **USD 655.5 billion by 2029**, underscoring the economic significance of AI in data processing.
- **Cloud Computing and Infrastructure:** AI is optimizing cloud infrastructure management, resource allocation, and energy efficiency. AI algorithms predict resource needs, automatically scale services, and identify potential bottlenecks, ensuring seamless operation of cloud platforms. Major cloud providers like Google, Amazon, and Microsoft leverage AI to manage their vast data centers, leading to significant energy savings and improved performance.
- **Cybersecurity:** AI plays a critical role in enhancing cybersecurity defenses. AI-powered systems can detect and respond to cyber threats in real-time by analyzing network traffic, identifying anomalous behavior, and predicting potential attacks. This proactive approach is essential in combating increasingly

sophisticated cyber threats. AI-driven cybersecurity solutions can detect **up to 95% of advanced persistent threats (APTs)** that traditional methods might miss.

- **Research and Development (R&D) in Tech:** AI is accelerating R&D across all technological domains. From designing new microchips to developing advanced robotics, AI simulations and generative models allow for rapid prototyping, testing, and optimization, drastically reducing development cycles and costs. This enables tech companies to innovate faster and bring cutting-edge products to market more quickly.
- **Personalized User Experiences:** AI is at the core of delivering highly personalized user experiences in tech products, from social media feeds and streaming services to e-commerce platforms. AI algorithms analyze user behavior, preferences, and interactions to tailor content, recommendations, and interfaces, leading to increased engagement and satisfaction. This personalization can lead to **a 10-30% increase in customer lifetime value** for tech companies.

Analysis of Benefits of the AI Revolution

The benefits of the AI revolution are far-reaching and can be summarized across several key dimensions:

- **Increased Efficiency and Productivity:** AI automates repetitive and time-consuming tasks, freeing up human workers to focus on more complex, creative, and strategic activities. This leads to significant gains in operational efficiency and overall productivity across industries. For example, automation in business processes can lead to **cost savings of 15-30%**.

- **Innovation and New Capabilities:** AI is a catalyst for innovation, enabling the creation of entirely new products, services, and business models that were previously unimaginable. From autonomous vehicles to generative art, AI is pushing the boundaries of what is technologically possible.
- **Cost Reduction:** By automating tasks, optimizing processes, and improving resource allocation, AI contributes to significant cost reductions for businesses. This can lead to higher profitability and more competitive pricing for consumers.
- **Improved Accuracy and Quality:** AI systems, when properly trained, can perform tasks with a high degree of accuracy and consistency, reducing errors and improving the quality of products and services. This is particularly evident in areas like medical diagnostics and manufacturing quality control.
- **Personalization and Customization:** AI enables unprecedented levels of personalization, tailoring experiences, products, and services to individual preferences. This enhances user satisfaction and creates stronger customer relationships.

In conclusion, the AI revolution is a powerful force for change, driving economic growth, fostering innovation, and transforming industries and human lives. While challenges and ethical considerations remain, the quantitative benefits and transformative potential of AI underscore its pivotal role in shaping the world today and in the future. Its impact on the technology industry, in particular, is profound, as AI becomes an integral part of how technology is built, managed, and delivered.

AI GOVERNANCE
AND REGULATION
KEY CONCERNS
Ethical Risks
Safety & Security
Bias & Fairness
CURRENT INITIATIVES
AI
EU AI Act
NIST AI RMF
AI Safety Institutes
FUTURE CHALLENGES & DIRECTIONS
• Harmonizinig global regulations
• Balancing innovation and oversight
• Addressing unforeseen AI risks
• Ensuring accountability and transparency

CHAPTER 4

AI GOVERNANCE AND REGULATIONS: NAVIGATING THE FUTURE OF INTELLIGENCE

As artificial intelligence rapidly evolves and integrates into the fabric of global society, the imperative for robust governance and effective regulation becomes increasingly critical. This chapter delves into the multifaceted landscape of AI governance, exploring the ethical principles, standards for addressing bias, and the regulatory frameworks essential for guiding AI evolution responsibly. We will also examine the contrasting philosophies of Open AI and Controlled AI, and analyze the diverse approaches to AI regulation across key regions: the United States, Europe, Russia, and Asia.

Ethics, Bias, and Regulatory Standards for AI Evolution

The responsible development and deployment of AI necessitates a strong foundation of ethical principles and clear regulatory standards. These are crucial to ensure that AI systems serve humanity beneficially, equitably, and safely.

Ethical Principles for AI

Several core ethical principles are widely recognized as fundamental for guiding AI development:

- **Fairness and Non-discrimination:** AI systems should be designed and used in a way that avoids and mitigates bias, ensuring equitable treatment and outcomes for all individuals and groups. This means actively addressing algorithmic bias stemming from skewed datasets or model design flaws.
- **Transparency and Explainability (XAI):** The decision-making processes of AI systems should be understandable and interpretable to humans, especially in high-stakes applications. This allows for accountability, auditing, and the identification of errors or biases. The concept of Explainable AI (XAI) is crucial here, aiming to make complex AI models more transparent.
- **Accountability and Responsibility:** Clear lines of responsibility must be established for the design, development, deployment, and use of AI systems. When AI systems cause harm or make errors, it should be possible to identify who is accountable.
- **Privacy and Data Governance:** Given AI's reliance on vast datasets, robust mechanisms for data privacy, security, and

ethical data governance are essential. This includes informed consent for data collection, secure data storage, and protection against unauthorized access or misuse.

- **Safety and Robustness:** AI systems must be designed to be safe, reliable, and robust, performing as intended even in unforeseen circumstances. This is particularly critical for AI in autonomous systems, healthcare, and critical infrastructure.
- **Human Oversight and Control:** Humans should retain ultimate control over AI systems, especially in critical decision-making processes. AI should augment human capabilities, not replace human judgment entirely.
- **Beneficence and Sustainability:** AI development should aim to benefit humanity and contribute to sustainable development, addressing global challenges such as climate change, poverty, and disease.

Addressing Bias in AI

Bias in AI is a pervasive and critical ethical challenge. It can manifest in various forms, including historical bias (reflecting societal prejudices in data), measurement bias (due to flawed data collection), and algorithmic bias (introduced during model design or training). Mitigating bias requires a systematic approach:

- **Diverse and Representative Datasets:** Actively curating and utilizing training datasets that are diverse and representative of the populations the AI system will interact with is fundamental. This helps prevent the AI from learning and perpetuating existing societal biases.

- **Bias Detection and Mitigation Techniques:** Employing specialized algorithms and methodologies to detect and quantify bias within AI models. Once detected, various techniques can be applied to mitigate bias, such as re-weighting training data, adjusting model parameters, or post-processing model outputs.
- **Fairness Metrics:** Developing and applying quantitative fairness metrics to evaluate AI system performance across different demographic groups. This allows for a measurable assessment of fairness and helps in identifying areas for improvement.
- **Ethical AI Review Boards:** Establishing interdisciplinary review boards comprising ethicists, legal experts, technologists, and social scientists to assess AI systems for potential biases and ethical risks before deployment.

Regulatory Standards for AI

Regulatory standards are emerging globally to translate ethical principles into actionable legal and policy frameworks. These standards aim to provide clarity, ensure compliance, and foster public trust in AI.

- **Risk-Based Approach:** Many proposed regulations adopt a risk-based approach, categorizing AI systems based on their potential to cause harm. Higher-risk AI applications (e.g., in critical infrastructure, law enforcement, or healthcare) face stricter regulations and oversight.
- **Data Governance and Privacy Regulations:** Existing data protection laws (like GDPR) are being extended or adapted to address AI-specific data challenges, focusing on data quality, consent, transparency in data usage, and data security.

- **Conformity Assessments and Audits:** Requiring AI systems, especially high-risk ones, to undergo conformity assessments, audits, and impact assessments to ensure compliance with regulatory requirements and ethical guidelines.
- **Post-Market Monitoring:** Implementing mechanisms for continuous monitoring of AI systems after deployment to detect and address any unforeseen risks, biases, or performance degradation.
- **Standardization:** Promoting the development of technical standards for AI, covering areas such as interoperability, data formats, testing methodologies, and security protocols.

Open AI vs. Controlled AI Approaches

The landscape of AI development is broadly characterized by two contrasting approaches: Open AI (often synonymous with open-source AI) and Controlled AI (or closed-source AI). These approaches differ fundamentally in their philosophy, accessibility, and implications for innovation, safety, and governance.

Open AI (Open-Source AI)

Open AI refers to AI models, algorithms, and software whose source code, training data, and sometimes even model weights are publicly available. This transparency allows anyone to access, inspect, modify, and distribute the technology. The philosophy behind Open AI emphasizes collaboration, rapid innovation, and democratic access to powerful AI tools.

Key Characteristics:

- **Transparency:** The inner workings of the AI are visible, allowing researchers, developers, and the public to understand how decisions are made, identify biases, and verify functionality.
- **Community Collaboration:** A global community of developers and researchers can contribute to improving the AI, leading to faster iteration, bug fixes, and diverse applications.
- **Accessibility and Democratization:** Open AI lowers the barrier to entry for AI development and deployment, enabling smaller organizations, startups, and individuals to leverage advanced AI capabilities without proprietary licenses.
- **Customization and Flexibility:** Users can adapt and fine-tune open models for specific tasks or integrate them into their existing systems.
- **Security through Scrutiny:** While seemingly counterintuitive, the open nature allows for widespread scrutiny, which can lead to quicker identification and patching of vulnerabilities.

Examples: TensorFlow, PyTorch (though these are frameworks, many models built on them are open-source), Hugging Face models, various open-source large language models (LLMs) like Llama 2.

Controlled AI (Closed-Source AI)

Controlled AI refers to proprietary AI models and systems whose source code, architecture, training data, and often model weights are kept private by the developing entity. Access and usage are typically governed by licenses, APIs, and terms of service. This approach prioritizes intellectual property protection, commercial control, and often, a more curated development environment.

Key Characteristics:

- **Proprietary Control:** The developing company maintains exclusive control over the AI, its development roadmap, and its commercialization.
- **Security by Obscurity (and Design):** While not a primary security measure, the private nature of the code can make it harder for malicious actors to identify vulnerabilities. Security is often a core design principle, with dedicated teams ensuring robustness.
- **Quality Assurance and Support:** Commercial entities often provide dedicated support, regular updates, and rigorous quality assurance for their controlled AI products.
- **Monetization:** This model allows companies to monetize their AI innovations through licensing, subscription services, or integration into their products.
- **Reduced Risk of Misuse (in theory):** Proponents argue that controlling access can mitigate the risk of malicious use of powerful AI models, though this is a contentious point.

Examples: OpenAI's GPT series (though OpenAI has released some models as open-source, their most advanced models are typically closed-source), Google's Gemini, Anthropic's Claude, Amazon's Alexa.

Key Differences that Divide Them

The fundamental differences between Open AI and Controlled AI approaches stem from their core philosophies regarding access, control, and collaboration:

Feature	Open AI (Open-Source AI)	Controlled AI (Closed-Source AI)
Accessibility	Publicly available code, data, and models.	Proprietary; access controlled by the developing entity.
Transparency	High; internal workings can be inspected.	Low; internal workings are typically hidden.
Innovation Model	Collaborative, community-driven, rapid iteration.	Centralized, company-driven, often more controlled releases.
Customization	High; users can modify and fine-tune.	Limited; customization usually via APIs or specific features.
Security	Enhanced by community scrutiny; faster vulnerability fixes.	Relies on internal security teams; potential for hidden flaws.
Monetization	Indirect (e.g., services, support, complementary products).	Direct (e.g., licenses, subscriptions, integrated products).

Risk of Misuse	Higher potential for misuse due to broad access.	Lower potential for misuse due to controlled access (debated).
Accountability	Distributed across community; can be complex to pinpoint.	Clearer accountability with the developing entity.

The choice between open and controlled AI approaches often involves a trade-off between fostering widespread innovation and maintaining control over powerful, potentially sensitive technologies. The debate continues regarding which approach best serves the long-term interests of society and responsible AI development.

How Regulations are Impacting the AI Revolution Globally

Governments worldwide are actively developing and implementing regulatory frameworks to manage the opportunities and risks presented by AI. These regulations vary significantly based on regional priorities, legal traditions, and geopolitical considerations.

United States

The U.S. approach to AI regulation has historically been more fragmented and sector-specific, relying on existing laws and agency guidance rather than a single, comprehensive AI law. However, there is a growing push for more unified federal action.

- **Sector-Specific Regulation:** AI is currently regulated through existing laws related to privacy (e.g., HIPAA for healthcare, CCPA for California), consumer protection – Federal Trade Commission (FTC), and civil rights. For example, the Equal Employment Opportunity Commission (EEOC) has issued guidance on AI use in hiring to prevent discrimination.
- **Executive Orders and Initiatives:** White house administration has issued executive orders promoting responsible AI innovation and establishing a framework for federal agencies to develop AI policies. Including AI Policy "Winning the Race: America's AI Action Plan" which outlines over 90 policy actions. The National Institute of Standards and Technology (NIST) has released an AI Risk Management Framework to guide organizations in managing AI risks.
- **State-Level Initiatives:** Several states are enacting their own AI-related legislation, particularly concerning data privacy, facial recognition, and algorithmic transparency. This creates a complex patchwork of regulations across the country.
- **Focus Areas:** Key concerns in the U.S. include intellectual property rights (especially concerning generative AI and copyrighted works), national security implications, and ensuring fair and unbiased AI systems.
- **Impact:** The fragmented approach can foster innovation by allowing flexibility but also creates regulatory uncertainty and potential for inconsistent application of rules. The emphasis is often on voluntary frameworks and industry-led best practices, with a lean towards promoting innovation.

Europe

Europe has taken a leading role in comprehensive AI regulation with the development of the **EU AI Act**, which is poised to be the world's first comprehensive legal framework for AI. This Act adopts a risk-based approach.

- **EU AI Act:** This landmark legislation classifies AI systems into different risk categories (unacceptable, high, limited, minimal risk). Prohibited AI practices include social scoring by governments and real-time remote biometric identification in public spaces (with limited exceptions). High-risk AI systems face stringent requirements, including conformity assessments, risk management systems, data governance, transparency, human oversight, and cybersecurity measures.
- **GDPR (General Data Protection Regulation):** The GDPR already provides a strong foundation for data privacy, which significantly impacts AI development and deployment in Europe, particularly concerning the collection and processing of personal data for AI training.
- **Focus Areas:** The EU's primary focus is on protecting fundamental rights, ensuring safety, and fostering trust in AI. There is a strong emphasis on human-centric AI and ethical considerations.
- **Impact:** The EU AI Act is expected to set a global standard, influencing AI regulations in other jurisdictions (the "Brussels Effect"). It will likely increase compliance costs for businesses operating in or targeting the European market but aims to create a level playing field and promote responsible innovation.

Russia

Russia's approach to AI regulation is characterized by a strong emphasis on national security, technological sovereignty, and state control over critical technologies. While there isn't a single, overarching AI law akin to the EU AI Act, Russia has been developing a strategic framework.

- **National Strategy for AI Development:** Russia adopted a National Strategy for the Development of Artificial Intelligence until 2030, which outlines the country's goals for AI research, development, and application. The strategy emphasizes the creation of domestic AI technologies and reducing reliance on foreign solutions.
- **Experimental Legal Regimes:** Russia has introduced experimental legal regimes in certain regions (e.g., Moscow) to test and refine AI regulations, particularly for high-risk applications like autonomous vehicles and medical diagnostics. These regimes allow for a more flexible regulatory environment to foster innovation while monitoring risks.
- **Emphasis on State Control and Data Localization:** There is a strong focus on ensuring state control over AI systems and data, particularly for sensitive applications. Data localization requirements, which mandate that personal data of Russian citizens be stored on servers within Russia, significantly impact foreign AI companies operating in the country.
- **Ethical Guidelines:** Russia has also developed a National Code of Ethics in the Field of Artificial Intelligence, which outlines principles such as human-centricity, safety, transparency, and non-discrimination. However, the enforcement mechanisms for these ethical guidelines are still evolving.

- **Impact:** Russia's regulatory approach aims to accelerate domestic AI development and ensure national security interests are protected. This can lead to a more centralized and controlled AI ecosystem, potentially limiting the entry of foreign AI providers and fostering a distinct national AI landscape.

Asia

Asia presents a diverse regulatory landscape for AI, with countries like India, China, Singapore, and Japan adopting distinct approaches driven by their unique economic, political, and social contexts.

India

India's AI policy promotes AI Development, Adoption and responsible AI usage. IndiaAI Mission established in Mar 2024, provides 3 areas of focus to build and grow AI in India. Providing funding, building infrastructure and promoting skill development in AI.

Ministry of Electronics and Information Technology or MeitY of India has provided several guidance and guardrails to ensure AI development and usage is well governed. **MeitY** has also enabling AI adoption by providing datasets, models and uses cases to drive AI Innovation in the country. By doing this, they are ensuring governance is managed by government at the foundational level.

India's data protection act, DPDPA or **Digital Personal Data Project Act** is another significant decision made and provides a framework of data privacy in India. It provides guidance and outlines how personal data can be processed by both public and private entities, ensuring necessary governance.

China

China is a global leader in AI development and has adopted a comprehensive, yet often state-centric, regulatory approach.

Multi-pronged Regulatory Framework: China has introduced a series of regulations targeting specific AI applications, including deep synthesis technologies (e.g., deepfakes), algorithmic recommendation services, and generative AI. These regulations emphasize content moderation, data security, and algorithmic transparency.

Data Governance and Cybersecurity: China's Cybersecurity Law, Data Security Law, and Personal Information Protection Law (PIPL) form a robust framework for data governance, significantly impacting how AI models are trained and deployed, especially concerning personal data.

Algorithmic Accountability: Regulations require AI service providers to register their algorithms, conduct security assessments, and ensure that algorithms do not discriminate or harm national security or public interest.

State-led Development: The Chinese government plays a significant role in directing AI research and development, often through national plans and substantial investments, aiming to achieve global leadership in AI by 2030.

Impact: China's regulations aim to balance innovation with social stability and state control. The strict data and content regulations can pose challenges for foreign companies but also create a more controlled environment for domestic AI development.

Singapore

Singapore has adopted a pro-innovation and governance-focused approach, aiming to be a trusted hub for AI development.

- **Model AI Governance Framework:** Singapore has developed a Model AI Governance Framework, which provides practical guidance for organizations in designing, developing, and deploying AI solutions responsibly. It focuses on explainability, fairness, ethics, and accountability.
- **AI Verify:** Singapore launched AI Verify, an AI governance testing framework and software toolkit that allows companies to conduct technical tests on their AI systems and disclose their performance against various ethical principles.
- **Light-Touch Regulation:** Singapore generally favors a more agile and less prescriptive regulatory approach, focusing on voluntary adoption of best practices and industry-led initiatives, with regulations introduced only when necessary.
- **Impact:** Singapore's approach aims to foster a vibrant AI ecosystem by providing clarity and trust, attracting AI talent and investment while ensuring responsible AI development.

Japan

Japan's approach to AI regulation is characterized by a focus on human-centric AI, international collaboration, and promoting data free flow with trust.

- **Human-Centric AI Principles:** Japan has adopted principles for AI development that emphasize human dignity, diversity, and sustainable development. These principles guide policy-making and industry practices.
- **Data Free Flow with Trust (DFFT):** Japan actively promotes the concept of DFFT, advocating for international rules that facilitate cross-border data flows while ensuring data protection and trust. This stance influences its approach to AI data governance.
- **Copyright and AI Training:** Japan has a relatively liberal stance on copyright and AI training, allowing broad use of copyrighted works for information analysis, which can benefit AI model development. This can potentially change.
- **Impact:** Japan seeks to balance innovation with ethical considerations and international cooperation, aiming to be a leader in responsible AI development that aligns with democratic values.

Conclusion

The global landscape of AI governance and regulation is rapidly evolving, reflecting diverse national priorities and values. While there is a growing consensus on core ethical principles such as fairness, transparency, and accountability, the implementation of these principles varies significantly across regions. The ongoing debate between Open AI and Controlled AI approaches further highlights the fundamental choices societies face in shaping the future of artificial intelligence. As AI continues to advance, international dialogue and collaboration will be crucial to establish common ground, mitigate risks, and ensure that AI serves as a force for good, benefiting all of humanity.

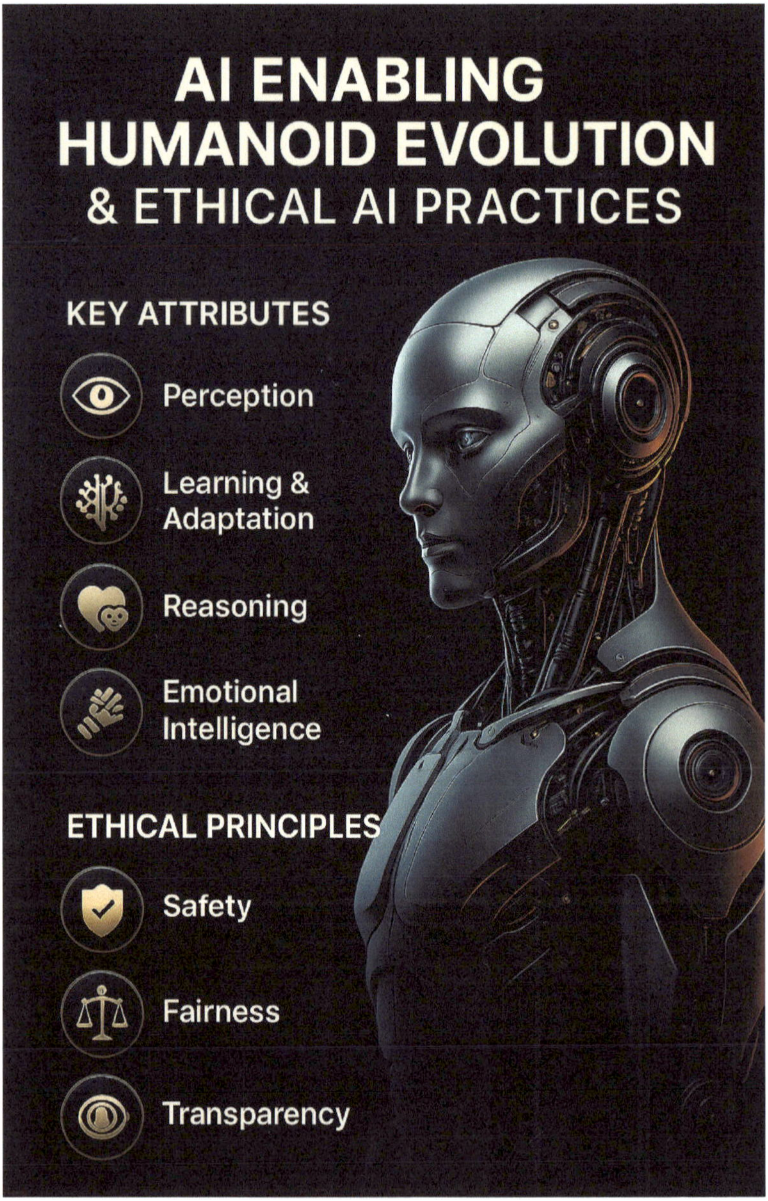
AI ENABLING
HUMANOID EVOLUTION
& ETHICAL AI PRACTICES
KEY ATTRIBUTES
Perception
Learning &
Adaptation
Reasoning
Emotional
Intelligence
ETHICAL PRINCIPLES
Safety
Fairness
Transparency

CHAPTER 5

AI, HUMANOID EVOLUTION, AND ETHICAL IMPERATIVES

The convergence of Artificial Intelligence and robotics is ushering in a new era: the evolution of humanoids. These machines, designed to resemble and interact with humans, are no longer confined to the realm of science fiction. AI is the driving force behind their increasing capabilities, enabling them to perceive, learn, reason, and adapt in ways that were once unimaginable. This chapter explores how AI is fundamentally enabling the evolution of humanoids and why it is critically important to ensure these advanced creations are built upon robust ethical AI practices.

How AI is Enabling Humanoid Evolution

The development of sophisticated humanoids is intrinsically linked to advancements in AI. AI provides the 'brain' that allows these physical forms to function intelligently, interact with their environment, and perform complex tasks. Several key areas of AI are crucial to this evolution:

1. Advanced Perception and Understanding

AI, particularly through **Computer Vision** and **Natural Language Processing (NLP)**, grants humanoids the ability to perceive and understand the world around them in a human-like manner. Computer vision allows humanoids to interpret visual information from cameras, recognizing objects, faces, gestures, and navigating complex environments. NLP enables them to understand spoken and written human language, engage in natural conversations, and process contextual cues. This perception is vital for humanoids to operate effectively in human-centric environments.

2. Learning and Adaptation

Machine Learning (ML) and **Deep Learning (DL)** are at the core of humanoid evolution, allowing them to learn from data and experience. Through reinforcement learning, humanoids can learn to perform complex motor skills, adapt to new situations, and refine their actions over time. For instance, a humanoid might learn to walk on uneven terrain or manipulate delicate objects through trial and error, guided by AI algorithms. This learning capability makes humanoids increasingly versatile and capable of handling unforeseen circumstances.

3. Reasoning and Decision-Making

AI provides humanoids with the capacity for reasoning and decision-making. Beyond simple programmed responses, advanced AI enables humanoids to analyze situations, infer solutions, and make choices that align with their objectives. This is crucial for autonomous operation in dynamic environments, allowing humanoids to prioritize tasks, resolve conflicts, and respond intelligently to human commands or environmental changes.

4. Human-Robot Interaction and Emotional Intelligence

For humanoids to seamlessly integrate into human society, they need to understand and respond to human emotions and social cues. AI is enabling this through the development of **Emotional AI**, which allows humanoids to detect and interpret human emotions from facial expressions, tone of voice, and body language. This capability facilitates more natural and empathetic interactions, making humanoids more acceptable and effective in roles requiring social engagement, such as caregiving or customer service.

5. Dexterity and Manipulation

While robotics provides the physical mechanisms, AI algorithms are essential for controlling the fine motor skills and dexterity required for humanoids to perform intricate tasks. AI-powered control systems enable humanoids to grasp and manipulate objects with precision, perform delicate operations, and adapt their movements to varying object properties. This is critical for applications in manufacturing, healthcare, and domestic assistance.

The Criticality of Ethical AI Practices in Humanoid Development

As humanoids become more sophisticated and integrated into daily life, the ethical considerations surrounding their development and deployment become paramount. Building humanoids on strong ethical AI practices is not merely a matter of compliance but a fundamental necessity to ensure their safe, beneficial, and equitable integration into society. The risks associated with unethical AI in humanoids are amplified due to their physical presence and potential for direct interaction with humans.

1. Preventing Bias and Discrimination

Humanoids, like any AI system, learn from data. If the data used to train their AI systems is biased (e.g., reflecting societal prejudices in gender, race, or socioeconomic status), the humanoids can perpetuate and even amplify these biases in their interactions and decision-making. This could lead to discriminatory behavior in critical applications like law enforcement, healthcare, or employment. Ethical AI practices require rigorous efforts to identify and mitigate bias in training data and algorithms, ensuring humanoids treat all individuals fairly and equitably.

2. Ensuring Safety and Reliability

Given their physical form and potential for autonomous action, the safety and reliability of humanoids are non-negotiable. Unethical or poorly designed AI could lead to unpredictable or harmful behavior, posing risks to human safety. Ethical AI development requires robust testing, verification, and validation processes to ensure humanoids operate reliably and safely in all intended environments. This also includes designing fail-safe mechanisms and clear protocols for human oversight and intervention.

3. Transparency and Explainability

As humanoids make increasingly complex decisions, it is crucial to understand how and why they arrive at certain conclusions. Lack of transparency (the "black box" problem) can hinder accountability and trust. Ethical AI practices advocate for explainable AI (XAI) in humanoids, allowing developers and users to understand the reasoning behind their actions, especially in high-stakes situations. This transparency is vital for debugging, auditing, and building public confidence.

4. Privacy and Data Security

Humanoids, particularly those designed for personal assistance or social interaction, will inevitably collect vast amounts of personal data, including sensitive information about individuals and their environments. Unethical data practices could lead to privacy breaches, misuse of personal information, or surveillance. Ethical AI development for humanoids must prioritize robust data security measures, transparent data collection policies, and strict adherence to privacy regulations, ensuring that individuals retain control over their data.

5. Accountability and Responsibility

When a humanoid makes an error or causes harm, determining accountability can be complex. Is it the fault of the designer, the programmer, the operator, or the AI itself? Ethical AI frameworks seek to establish clear lines of responsibility and accountability for the actions of humanoids. This involves legal and ethical guidelines that define who is responsible for the humanoid's behavior and how redress can be sought in cases of harm.

6. Impact on Human Dignity and Autonomy

The increasing sophistication of humanoids raises philosophical questions about their impact on human dignity and autonomy. Over reliance on humanoids for decision-making or care could diminish human capabilities or create unhealthy dependencies. Ethical considerations must guide the design of humanoids to augment, rather than replace, human capabilities, and to respect human autonomy and dignity in all interactions.

7. Preventing Misuse and Malicious Applications

Humanoids, like any powerful technology, could be misused for malicious purposes, such as surveillance, manipulation, or autonomous weaponry. Ethical AI practices must include safeguards against such misuse, promoting the development of humanoids solely for beneficial applications and advocating for international regulations to prevent their weaponization or deployment in ways that violate human rights.

Conclusion

AI is undeniably the engine driving the rapid evolution of humanoids, transforming them from futuristic concepts into tangible realities. From enhanced perception and learning to sophisticated human-robot interaction, AI is Instilling these machines with capabilities that promise to reshape industries and daily life. However, this transformative potential comes with profound ethical responsibilities. Ensuring humanoids are built on ethical AI foundations that ensures fairness, safety, transparency, privacy, accountability, and respect for human dignity is highly critical. It is not just a moral imperative but a critical step towards realizing a future where humanoids serve humanity responsibly and beneficially. Without a strong ethical compass, the evolution of humanoids risks exacerbating societal inequalities and introducing unforeseen dangers.

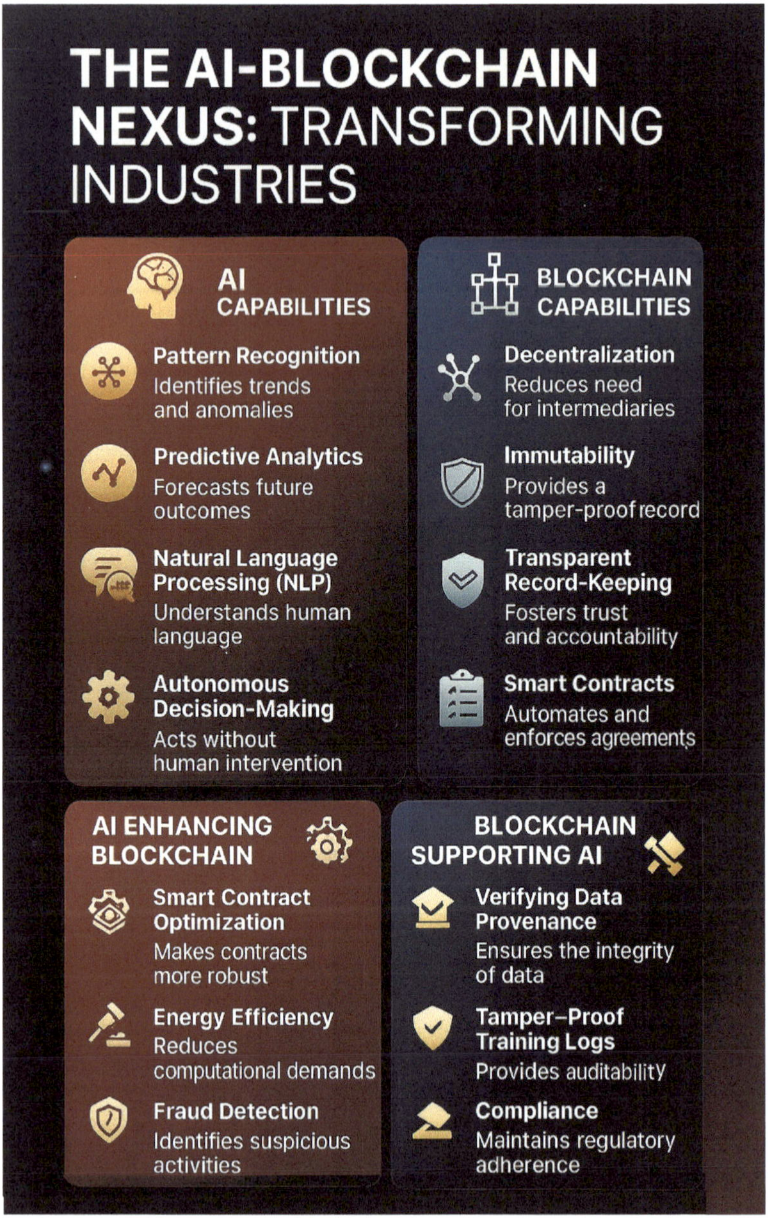
THE AI-BLOCKCHAIN NEXUS: TRANSFORMING INDUSTRIES
AI CAPABILITIES
Pattern Recognition
Identifies trends and anomalies
Predictive Analytics
Forecasts future outcomes
Natural Language Processing (NLP)
Understands human language
Autonomous Decision-Making
Acts without human intervention
BLOCKCHAIN CAPABILITIES
Decentralization
Reduces need for intermediaries
Immutability
Provides a tamper-proof record
Transparent Record-Keeping
Fosters trust and accountability
Smart Contracts
Automates and enforces agreements
AI ENHANCING BLOCKCHAIN
Smart Contract Optimization
Makes contracts more robust
Energy Efficiency
Reduces computational demands
Fraud Detection
Identifies suspicious activities
BLOCKCHAIN SUPPORTING AI
Verifying Data Provenance
Ensures the integrity of data
Tamper–Proof Training Logs
Provides auditability
Compliance
Maintains regulatory adherence

CHAPTER 6

THE AI-BLOCKCHAIN NEXUS: TRANSFORMING INDUSTRIES

Artificial Intelligence (AI) and Blockchain are two of the most transformative technologies of the 21st century. Separately, they have driven innovation across industries, but when combined, their potential multiplies. This chapter explores how AI is enhancing blockchain technology and how their integration is solving real world problems in various sectors such as finance, healthcare, supply chain, and real estate.

1. Understanding the Foundation: What AI and Blockchain Bring Individually

AI Capabilities

AI, at its core, excels in tasks that require cognitive simulation. Its key capabilities include:

- **Pattern Recognition:** Identifying trends and anomalies in vast datasets, crucial for predictive analytics and fraud detection.

- **Predictive Analytics:** Forecasting future outcomes based on historical data, enabling proactive decision-making.
- **Natural Language Processing (NLP):** Understanding, interpreting, and generating human language, facilitating human-machine interaction and data extraction from unstructured text.
- **Autonomous Decision-Making:** Making choices and taking actions without direct human intervention, based on learned rules and real-time data.

Blockchain Capabilities

Blockchain technology provides a robust framework for secure and transparent data management. Its fundamental capabilities are:

- **Decentralization:** Distributing data across a network, eliminating the need for a central authority and reducing single points of failure.
- **Immutability:** Ensuring that once data is recorded on the blockchain, it cannot be altered or deleted, providing a tamper-proof record.
- **Transparent Record-Keeping:** All participants in the network can view transactions, fostering trust and accountability.
- **Smart Contracts:** Self-executing contracts with the terms of the agreement directly written into code, automating processes and ensuring compliance.

2. AI Enhancing Blockchain Technology

The synergy between AI and Blockchain allows AI to address some of Blockchain's inherent challenges while significantly augmenting its capabilities:

2.1 Smart Contract Optimization

AI plays a crucial role in making smart contracts more intelligent and robust. AI enables:

- **Detection of vulnerabilities in smart contracts:** AI algorithms can analyze smart contract code to identify potential bugs, security flaws, or logical errors before deployment.
- **Automated testing and simulation of contract scenarios:** AI can run numerous simulations to test contract behavior under various conditions, ensuring reliability and desired outcomes.
- **Predictive logic for self-evolving contract terms:** AI can be trained on historical blockchain data to automatically detect fraud-prone transactions and dynamically adjust smart contract rules to mitigate risks, making contracts more adaptive and secure.

2.2 Energy Efficiency in Consensus Mechanisms

Consensus mechanisms, particularly Proof-of-Work (PoW) used in some blockchains, are energy-intensive. AI can contribute to greater efficiency by:

- **Predicting optimal mining schedules:** AI can analyze network conditions and energy costs to recommend the most efficient times for mining operations.

- **Improving consensus mechanisms:** AI can be used to design and optimize more energy-efficient consensus mechanisms like Proof-of-Stake (PoS) or Delegated PoS, reducing the computational burden.
- **Minimizing redundant calculations:** AI can help streamline the mining process by identifying and minimizing unnecessary computations.

2.3 Fraud Detection and Security

AI adds an advanced layer of security and fraud detection to blockchain networks:

- **Monitoring blockchain activity in real-time:** AI systems can continuously analyze transaction flows and network behavior.
- **Detecting abnormal patterns:** AI can identify unusual transaction volumes, sudden spikes in wallet activity, or other deviations from normal behavior that might indicate malicious intent.
- **Training anomaly detection models:** Machine learning models can be trained to flag suspicious activities and potential cyberattacks early, enhancing the overall integrity and security of the blockchain network.

3. Blockchain Supporting AI: Data Integrity and Trust

High-quality, trustworthy data is paramount for effective AI models. Blockchain provides the necessary infrastructure to ensure data integrity and build trust in AI systems:

- **Verifying the provenance of data:** Blockchain can create an immutable record of data origin, ensuring that the data used to train AI models is authentic and untampered.
- **Storing tamper-proof logs of training data:** Every step of an AI model's training process, including the datasets used, can be logged on a blockchain, providing an auditable and verifiable history.
- **Ensuring compliance with data regulations:** Blockchain's transparent and immutable nature can help AI systems comply with stringent data regulations like GDPR and HIPAA by providing verifiable proof of data handling and consent. This is essential for building trustworthy AI, especially in sensitive industries like healthcare and finance.

4. Industry Applications: AI + Blockchain in Action

The integration of AI and Blockchain is driving transformative changes across various industries:

4.1 Financial Services

Use Case: AI-driven credit scoring with blockchain-backed identity verification.

Benefit: Enables real-time loan approvals, reduces fraud, and creates more robust Know Your Customer (KYC) systems by securely verifying identities and financial histories.

4.2 Healthcare

Use Case: AI models trained on patient data stored on blockchain networks.

Benefit: Facilitates personalized treatments, ensures secure and interoperable patient records across different healthcare providers, and enhances data privacy.

4.3 Supply Chain

Use Case: AI monitors and predicts supply-demand trends, while blockchain ensures auditability and transparency of goods movement.

Benefit: Leads to transparent logistics, effective counterfeit prevention, reduced delays, and optimized inventory management by providing real-time, verifiable data on product journeys.

4.4 Real Estate

Use Case: Blockchain-based land registries combined with AI for property valuation and investment insights.

Benefit: Provides instant ownership verification, streamlines property transactions, and enables smarter real estate investing through AI-driven market analysis.

4.5 Insurance

Use Case: AI automates claims processing while blockchain maintains a secure and immutable claim ledger.

Benefit: Significantly reduces fraud, accelerates claim settlement times, and enhances transparency in the insurance process.

4.6 Other Industries

Beyond these, the AI-Blockchain nexus is impacting other sectors:

- **Energy:** AI optimizes energy consumption and distribution on smart grids, with blockchain securing energy trading and ensuring transparent billing.
- **Government & Public Services:** AI enhances efficiency in public administration, while blockchain secures digital identities and voting systems.
- **Media & Entertainment:** AI assists in content creation and personalization, with blockchain ensuring intellectual property rights and transparent royalty distribution.

5. Technical Synergies and Emerging Patterns

The combination of AI and Blockchain creates powerful technical synergies:

AI Capability	Blockchain Complement	Result
Predictive Analytics	Immutable Data Records	Forecasting with trusted data
NLP	Smart Contract Generation	Human-readable and automated agreements
Reinforcement Learning	Dynamic Smart Contracts	Self-optimizing and adaptive protocols
Computer Vision	Asset Verification (e.g., NFTs)	Automated digital asset valuation and authenticity checks

6. The Road Ahead: Future Trends

The convergence of AI and Blockchain is still in its early stages, but several promising future trends are emerging:

- **Decentralized AI Marketplaces:** Platforms where AI models and data are traded transparently and securely using blockchain technology, fostering innovation and fair compensation.
- **AI-Powered DAOs (Decentralized Autonomous Organizations):** AI models could enhance the governance of DAOs, enabling smarter, more efficient, and truly autonomous decision-making with minimal human intervention.
- **Self-Regulating Systems:** AI models, leveraging blockchain's immutable data, could evolve and audit themselves in real-time, ensuring compliance and ethical operation without constant human oversight.
- **Enhanced Data Privacy and Security:** The combination will lead to more robust solutions for privacy-preserving AI, such as federated learning on blockchain, where models are trained on decentralized data without exposing raw information.

Conclusion

The convergence of AI and blockchain represents a paradigm shift. Together, they enable systems that are not only intelligent but also secure, transparent, and highly efficient. As industries increasingly adopt this dual-stack architecture, we are witnessing the early signs of a more automated, accountable, and efficient future. This powerful combination holds the key to unlocking new levels of trust, automation, and innovation across the global economy, fundamentally transforming how we interact with data, systems, and each other.

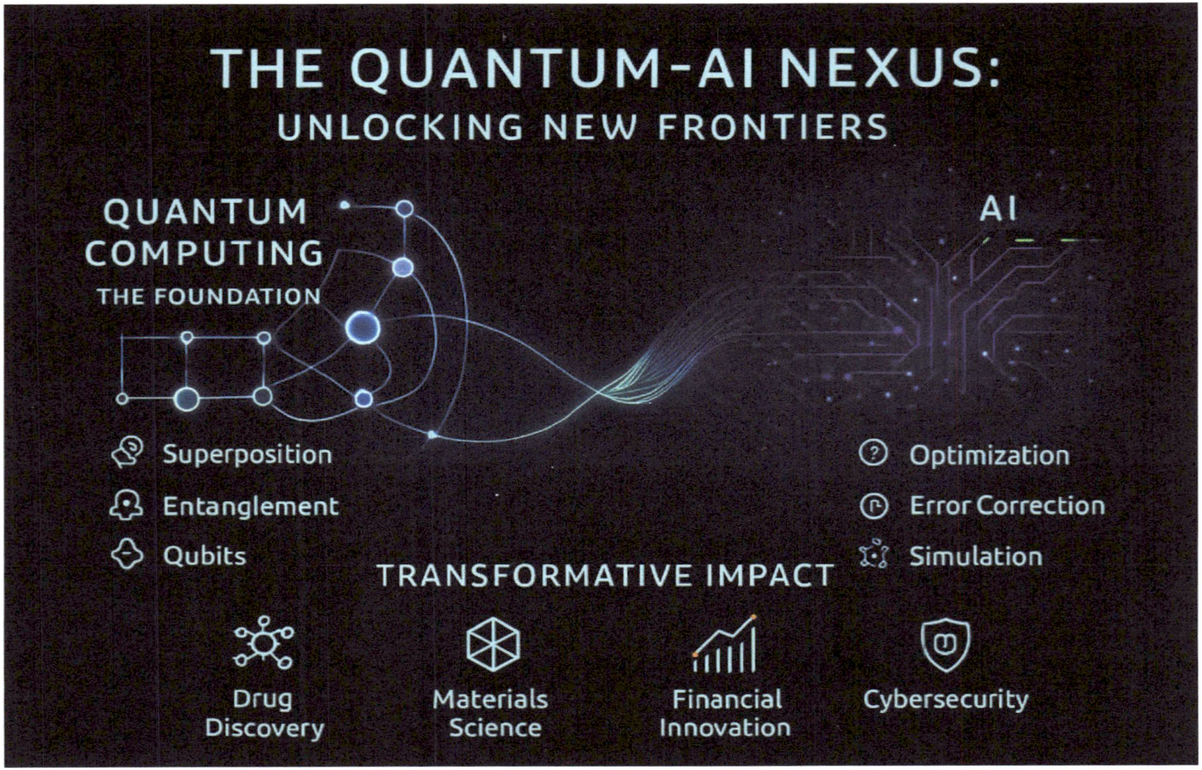
THE QUANTUM-AI NEXUS:
UNLOCKING NEW FRONTIERS
QUANTUM COMPUTING
THE FOUNDATION
Superposition
Entanglement
Qubits
AI
Optimization
Error Correction
Simulation
TRANSFORMATIVE IMPACT
Drug Discovery
Materials Science
Financial Innovation
Cybersecurity

CHAPTER 7

AI IN QUANTUM COMPUTING

Quantum computing is one of the most exciting and potentially game changing technologies of our time. Unlike traditional computers, which process data in bits (zeros and ones), quantum computers use a completely new concepts: qubits. These quantum bits can exist in multiple states simultaneously, thanks to the laws of quantum physics. This capability allows quantum computers to perform many calculations at once, promising to solve problems that are far too complex for today's computers, like modeling molecules for drug discovery, optimizing massive logistics networks, or predicting financial markets.

However, building, controlling, and programming these delicate quantum systems is incredibly challenging. This is where Artificial Intelligence (AI) plays a crucial role. AI patterns, making predictions, and automating difficult task makes quantum technology more powerful and accessible. In this chapter we will explore how AI is instrumental in advancing the quantum computing technology and innovation, and delves into the transformative use cases and profound benefits that arise from their powerful integrations.

1. Quantum Basics in Simple Terms

To understand the synergy between AI and quantum computing, it's helpful to grasp a few fundamental quantum concepts:

What Is a Qubit?

A qubit (quantum bit) is the smallest unit of data in a quantum computer. Unlike a regular bit that's either a 0 or a 1, a qubit can be both at the same time, a phenomenon known as superposition. This ability allows quantum computers to perform many calculations simultaneously, offering a significant advantage over classical computers. Imagine flipping a coin: a classical bit is like a coin landing on heads or tails, while a qubit is like a coin spinning in the air, both heads and tails at the same time until observed.

What Is Gate Fidelity?

Quantum computers use quantum gates to perform operations on qubits, similar to logic gates in classical computing. Gate fidelity measures how accurately these operations are performed. Think of it like a recipe: if a chef follows a recipe exactly, the dish turns out perfect. Gate fidelity tells us how closely the quantum computer follows the 'recipe' for a specific operation. Low fidelity means errors; high fidelity means precision, which is crucial for reliable quantum computations.

What Is Bayesian Optimization?

Bayesian optimization is a smart way for AI to make decisions when testing something is expensive or slow, like tuning a quantum machine. Instead of trying every possible adjustment, Bayesian optimization listens to each outcome and learns which adjustment is likely to lead to the best result, saving time and effort. This method is particularly useful for fine-tuning the complex parameters of quantum hardware.

2. How AI Improves Quantum Computing

AI is emerging as a critical tool to overcome the immense challenges in building, controlling, and programming quantum systems:

2.1 Designing Better Quantum Circuits

AI helps in the complex task of designing stable and scalable quantum hardware and software by:

- **Optimizing Qubit Layout and Connectivity:** AI algorithms can analyze various qubit arrangements and interconnections to identify configurations that minimize errors and maximize computational efficiency.
- **Suggesting Optimal Circuit Designs:** AI can use trial-and-error learning (like reinforcement learning) to find better ways to arrange operations using fewer steps (fewer gates), leading to more efficient quantum programs.
- **Reducing Errors in Layout:** AI can optimize how quantum circuits are laid out on real hardware, reducing the potential for errors during execution.

2.2 Detecting and Correcting Errors

Quantum systems are highly susceptible to noise and errors. AI is vital for addressing these challenges:

- **Spotting Error Patterns:** AI helps by spotting patterns in how and when errors happen, allowing for more effective error mitigation strategies.
- **Predicting System Failures:** AI can predict which parts of the quantum system are likely to fail, enabling proactive maintenance and adjustments.
- **Assisting in Automatic Error Correction:** AI assists in developing and implementing automatic error correction strategies before failures occur, maintaining quantum coherence and computation integrity.

2.3 Smart Control and Calibration

Maintaining the delicate quantum state of qubits requires precise calibration and control. AI is indispensable here:

- **Continuous Hardware Adjustment:** AI helps by continuously adjusting hardware settings using techniques like Bayesian optimization, learning over time which tuning methods work best.
- **Improved Qubit Control:** AI improves how qubits are controlled and connected for better performance, ensuring the stability and fidelity of quantum operations.
- **Automated Calibration:** AI systems can automate the complex and time-consuming process of calibrating quantum processors, adjusting parameters to ensure optimal performance.

2.4 Accelerating Quantum Simulations

AI can significantly speed up quantum simulations, which are crucial for scientific discovery:

- **Speeding Up Calculations:** AI helps by speeding up calculations by predicting parts of the simulation, reducing the computational load.
- **Reducing Measurement Needs:** AI can reduce the number of times a quantum system must be measured, which is a time-consuming process.
- **Exploring New Materials and Drugs:** AI assists scientists in exploring new materials and drug combinations by quickly simulating their quantum behavior, leading to faster discovery.

2.5 Optimizing Quantum Code (Quantum Compilation)

Translating high-level quantum algorithms into instructions executable on specific quantum hardware is a challenging compilation problem. AI can streamline this process:

- **Choosing Best Translation Paths:** AI helps choose the best translation path for quantum code, optimizing it for specific hardware architectures.
- **Reducing Execution Time and Energy:** AI can reduce the time and energy needed to run quantum programs by optimizing the compilation process.
- **Adapting to Hardware:** AI assists in adapting quantum programs to different types of quantum hardware, ensuring compatibility and efficiency.

3. Use Cases Where AI and Quantum Work Together

The integration of AI into the quantum computing ecosystem offers a multitude of benefits and opens up new avenues for innovation across various fields:

Drug Discovery

AI filters out millions of molecules to find promising candidates, while quantum computers then simulate how these molecules behave at the atomic level. This synergy leads to a faster and cheaper path to finding new medicines, accelerating the development of life-saving drugs.

Materials Design

AI suggests new materials with desired properties, and quantum systems simulate their behavior and verify performance at the quantum level. This enables the discovery of stronger, lighter, or more energy-efficient materials for various applications, from aerospace to electronics.

Quantum Machine Learning

Quantum computers may one day run AI models more efficiently than classical ones, processing and analyzing data in ways previously impossible. AI today helps design those models and makes them compatible with limited quantum hardware. This promises smarter algorithms for solving complex real-world problems like climate modeling or logistics optimization.

Financial Modeling and Optimization

Quantum AI can tackle highly complex optimization problems in finance, leading to more accurate risk assessment, portfolio optimization, and fraud detection. This includes developing more sophisticated trading strategies by analyzing vast market data with quantum machine learning, or optimizing complex financial derivatives pricing.

Cybersecurity and Cryptography

While quantum computers pose a potential threat to current cryptographic standards, quantum AI can also be used to develop new, quantum-resistant cryptographic methods and enhance cybersecurity defenses. This includes designing unbreakable encryption algorithms based on quantum principles, or using quantum machine learning to detect and neutralize sophisticated cyber threats.

4. Benefits of Integrating AI with Quantum Computing

The partnership between AI and quantum computing yields significant benefits:

AI Contribution	Quantum Benefit
Optimization models	Efficient quantum circuit layout
Reinforcement learning	Adaptive error mitigation
Surrogate models	Approximate complex quantum behaviors
Classification & Clustering	Identify quantum phases of matter
Data-driven calibration	Improved qubit stability and performance

Challenges and Outlook

Even with AI's help, quantum computing is still in its early days. The challenges include:

- **Qubit Stability:** Keeping qubits stable long enough to complete tasks is a major hurdle.
- **Scalability and Affordability:** Making quantum systems scalable and affordable for widespread use remains a significant challenge.
- **Hybrid Systems:** Seamlessly combining classical and quantum systems for practical applications requires further development.

Despite these challenges, the outlook is bright. As AI continues to help us design, debug, and scale quantum systems, we are getting closer to real-world breakthroughs in medicine, finance, energy, and many other fields.

Conclusion

AI and quantum computing are two powerful forces in modern technology. AI helps unlock the full potential of quantum computers by making them easier to use, more efficient, and more reliable. In return, quantum computing may one day transform AI itself by solving problems today's computers simply can't handle. The partnership between these technologies represents not just the next step in computing, it could be the leap that defines the future of science, innovation, and society. This symbiotic relationship will drive innovation across virtually every scientific and industrial domain, ushering in a future where previously intractable challenges become solvable, and new frontiers of discovery are opened.

AI in HEALTHCARE and PHARMA INDUSTRIES

Transforming Lives

AI in Healthcare

- Assisting medical professionals in diagnosis
- Real-time analysis of electronic health records
- Automation of medical billing and coding
- Monitoring medical waste management
- Predictive diagnosis for wellness and fitness

AI in Pharmaceuticals

- Accelerating drug discovery
- Optimizing clinical trial design and recruitment
- Streamlining drug manufacturing processes

AI in Life Sciences & Regulations

- Enabling genomic data analysis and research

CHAPTER 8

AI IN HEALTHCARE, PHARMA, AND LIFE SCIENCES

Artificial Intelligence is rapidly reshaping the landscape of healthcare and the pharmaceutical industry, offering unprecedented opportunities to improve patient care, accelerate drug discovery, enhance operational efficiency, and personalize treatment approaches. From assisting medical professionals in diagnosis to streamlining complex drug development processes, AI's impact is profound and multifaceted. This chapter delves into the specific ways AI is revolutionizing various sectors within healthcare and pharmaceuticals, including its impact on research institutes and regulatory bodies.

AI in Healthcare

AI's influence spans across the entire healthcare ecosystem, from direct patient care to administrative efficiencies and technological advancements.

Healthcare Delivery and Operations

AI helps improve care and efficiency across healthcare providers, services, and facilities through:

- **Real-time analysis of electronic health records (EHRs)** for better diagnosis and treatment, often identifying subtle anomalies that might be missed by the human eye. For instance, AI algorithms can detect early signs of diseases such as cancer, diabetic retinopathy, or neurological disorders.
- **Automation of medical billing, coding, and insurance claims processing**, reducing administrative burdens and improving accuracy.
- **Monitoring and optimizing medical waste management and inventory systems**, leading to significant cost savings and improved operational efficiency.
- **AI-driven chatbots and virtual assistants** can handle routine patient inquiries, schedule appointments, and provide preliminary symptom assessment, freeing up human staff for more complex cases.
- **Clinical decision support systems** provide evidence-based recommendations to clinicians, thereby reducing medical errors and standardizing care.
- **Predicting patient admission rates**, so staff and resources are available when needed.
- **Monitoring cleanliness** using AI-powered robots that disinfect rooms and equipment.
- **Managing medical inventory** to ensure critical supplies are always stocked.

Example 1: Mayo Clinic, a world-renowned nonprofit academic medical center based in Rochester, Minnesota, uses AI for advanced clinical diagnosis and operational improvements. AI tools at Mayo assist in patient flow analysis, appointment scheduling, and billing accuracy, enhancing both care quality and operational efficiency.

Example 2: Mount Sinai Hospital in New York City uses AI to predict emergency room crowding and optimize patient movement, helping reduce wait times and improve treatment quality.

Health Technology and Medical Devices

AI is increasingly embedded within medical devices and digital health tools, enhancing their functionality, precision, and autonomy. These technologies improve medical care by analyzing real-time data, tracking chronic conditions, and guiding digital therapeutics.

- **Wearable devices integrated with AI** can continuously collect physiological data (heart rate, sleep patterns, activity levels) and use AI to detect deviations from baseline, alerting patients and providers to potential health issues.
- **Digital therapeutics**, which are software-based interventions, leverage AI to deliver personalized behavioral health programs, manage chronic conditions, and provide cognitive therapy.
- **Sophisticated health analytics platforms** aggregate and analyze vast datasets from electronic health records (EHRs), genomic data, and lifestyle information to provide actionable insights for population health management and individual wellness.

- **Medical imaging:** AI helps radiologists detect issues in X-rays, MRIs, and CT scans faster and more accurately.
- **Robotic surgery:** AI enhances robotic arms to assist in complex surgeries with greater precision. Adoption of robotic surgery is evolving fast, though still in early stages.
- **Implantable devices:** Smart pacemakers and insulin pumps adjust automatically based on the patient's real-time condition.

Example 1: TytoCare, headquartered in New York and Israel, developed an AI-powered remote exam kit allowing patients to conduct physical exams at home. Data is shared with healthcare providers for remote diagnosis, ideal for rural or quarantined settings.

Example 2: GE Healthcare offers AI-enabled ultrasound systems that assist clinicians, even those without deep imaging expertise in capturing better diagnostic images, which is especially valuable in rural and underserved regions.

Predictive Diagnosis for Wellness and Prevention

One of AI's most promising applications is in preventive healthcare, spotting risks before illness develops. By analyzing a combination of genetic predispositions, lifestyle data, environmental factors, and medical history, AI can identify individuals at high risk for developing certain diseases long before symptoms appear. This enables proactive interventions, preventive care, and personalized wellness plans. Few key areas currently available are

- **Predicting chronic diseases** like diabetes and heart failure by analyzing blood tests, vital signs, and lifestyle patterns.

- **Tracking behavior and activity** through fitness wearables and mobile apps.
- **Monitoring mental health** by analyzing tone, speech, or written text for signs of anxiety or depression.

Example: DeepMind Health, a division of Google, developed an AI model that can predict acute kidney injury (AKI) up to 48 hours in advance, giving doctors valuable time to prevent complications in high-risk patients.

AI in the Pharmaceutical Industry

AI is revolutionizing every stage of the pharmaceutical lifecycle, from drug discovery and development to manufacturing and post-market surveillance.

Drug Discovery and Development

The traditional process of drug discovery is notoriously long, expensive, and has a high failure rate. AI is revolutionizing this by significantly accelerating and de-risking various stages:

- **Target Identification and Validation:** AI algorithms can analyze vast biological datasets (genomic, proteomic, clinical) to identify novel disease targets and validate their relevance, speeding up the initial phase of drug discovery.
- **Molecule Generation and Optimization:** Generative AI models can design innovative chemical compounds with desired properties, predict their efficacy and toxicity, and optimize their structure for better binding to targets. This reduces the need for extensive wet-lab experimentation.

- **Drug Repurposing:** AI can identify existing drugs that could be repurposed for new diseases by analyzing molecular similarities and disease pathways, offering a faster route to new treatments.
- **Preclinical and Clinical Trial Optimization:** AI can predict the likelihood of success for drug candidates in clinical trials, identify suitable patient cohorts, and optimize trial design, leading to more efficient and cost-effective trials.

Example: Pfizer used AI in partnership with IBM Watson to identify antiviral compounds for COVID-19. This reduced the time needed to evaluate candidates in early-stage research.

Pharmaceutical Categories

AI's impact is felt across different types of pharmaceutical products:

- **Over-the-Counter (OTC) Drugs:** AI can analyze consumer behavior and market trends to predict demand for specific OTC products, optimizing supply chains and inventory management. AI-powered chatbots can provide personalized recommendations for OTC medications based on user-reported symptoms and health profiles, improving self-care guidance.

Usage: Predicting seasonal demand (e.g., flu outbreaks) and guiding customers to appropriate non-prescription remedies.

- **Generic Drugs:** AI can accelerate the development and approval of generic drugs by optimizing formulation processes and predicting bioequivalence. By analyzing vast datasets of chemical compounds and their properties, AI can identify optimal manufacturing parameters to ensure that generic versions are therapeutically equivalent to their brand name counterparts.

Usage: Maintaining quality control during manufacturing and simulating how generics compare to brand drugs in terms of absorption and effectiveness.

- **Biopharmaceuticals:** In the complex world of biopharmaceuticals (drugs derived from biological sources), AI is a game changer. AI algorithms can analyze intricate biological data, such as protein structures and genetic sequences, to identify new therapeutic targets and design new biological drugs (e.g., antibodies, vaccines). AI accelerates the development of cell and gene therapies by optimizing cell culture conditions and predicting therapeutic efficacy.

Usage: Identifying new biological targets and predicting protein structures (e.g., DeepMind's AlphaFold).

AI in Personalized Medicine and Diagnostics

Personalized medicine, which tailors medical treatment to the individual characteristics of each patient, is being significantly advanced by AI:

- **Genomic Analysis:** AI can rapidly analyze complex genomic data to identify genetic predispositions to diseases, predict drug responses, and guide personalized treatment strategies, particularly in oncology and rare diseases.
- **Precision Diagnostics:** AI-powered image analysis (e.g., for radiology, pathology, dermatology) can detect subtle anomalies

and patterns indicative of disease with high accuracy, often surpassing human capabilities. This leads to earlier and more precise diagnoses.

- **Predictive Analytics for Disease Progression:** AI models can predict disease progression, patient deterioration, or the risk of adverse events by analyzing electronic health records, lab results, and real-time physiological data, enabling proactive interventions.
- **Companion Diagnostics:** AI can help develop companion diagnostics that identify patients most likely to respond to a particular therapy, ensuring that the right treatment is given to the right patient.

AI in Life Sciences

AI's impact extends deeply into the broader life sciences, fundamentally changing how biological research is conducted and understood.

Genomics

AI plays a crucial role in interpreting the vast amounts of data generated by genomic sequencing. It can identify genetic variations, predict disease susceptibility, and understand gene function with unprecedented speed and accuracy.

Example: Illumina, a global leader in DNA sequencing technologies, is headquartered in San Diego, California. It uses AI to interpret genomic data more quickly and accurately, especially in oncology and rare genetic disease diagnostics.

Molecular Biology

AI is transforming molecular biology by enabling a deeper understanding of complex biological processes, particularly in protein structure prediction and function. CRISPR (Clustered Regularly Interspaced Short Palindromic Repeats) technology, for instance, benefits from AI in designing more precise gene-editing tools.

Example: DeepMind, an AI company owned by Alphabet Inc., developed AlphaFold, an AI system that accurately predicts protein structures transforming biological research worldwide.

Biochemistry and Drug Targeting

AI assists in analyzing biochemical reactions, identifying potential drug targets, and designing molecules that can interact with these targets effectively. This accelerates the early stages of drug discovery and development.

Example: The Broad Institute of MIT and Harvard applies AI to analyze biochemical reactions and support new therapeutic discoveries.

Accelerating Research and Collaboration

AI tools facilitate collaboration and accelerate research by enabling researchers to quickly access, analyze, and synthesize information from diverse sources. Natural Language Processing (NLP) tools, for instance, can analyze vast numbers of studies to identify patterns and new hypotheses, while data harmonization systems allow researchers across different labs to collaborate more effectively.

Example: BenevolentAI, headquartered in London, UK, uses AI to extract biomedical insights and uncover drug candidates. It collaborates with leading institutions to drive innovation in early-stage drug discovery.

AI's Role in Research Institutes and Regulatory Bodies

Beyond direct industry applications, AI is also transforming the operations and capabilities of research institutes and the regulatory bodies overseeing healthcare and pharmaceuticals.

Research Institutes

AI is empowering research institutes to conduct more efficient and impactful research. AI tools can analyze massive scientific literature databases to identify emerging trends, uncover hidden connections between research areas, and generate new hypotheses. In laboratories, AI automates data analysis from experiments, accelerates simulations, and manages complex research workflows. This allows researchers to focus on critical thinking and experimental design, speeding up the pace of scientific discovery in areas like genomics, proteomics, and personalized medicine.

Example: The National Institutes of Health (NIH) in the United States, the world's largest medical research agency, uses AI to model disease progression and analyze large-scale genomic data to advance treatments for cancer, Alzheimer's, and rare diseases.

Regulatory Agencies

Regulatory bodies like the FDA (U.S.), EMA (Europe), and PMDA (Japan) are increasingly leveraging AI to streamline processes, enhance oversight, and ensure the safety and efficacy of medical products. AI can assist in reviewing vast amounts of regulatory submissions, identifying inconsistencies or potential risks more quickly. AI powered tools can analyze real-world evidence (RWE) from electronic health records and insurance claims to monitor the post market safety and effectiveness of drugs and devices. This enables regulators to make more informed decisions, adapt to new technologies, and protect public health more effectively in an increasingly complex landscape.

Examples:

- **FDA (U.S. Food and Drug Administration):** Uses AI to monitor adverse drug reactions and automate document reviews.
- **EMA (European Medicines Agency):** Employs AI to improve safety signal detection in drug post-market surveillance.
- **PMDA (Pharmaceuticals and Medical Devices Agency, Japan):** Investigates the use of AI in clinical trial evaluation and regulatory science.

Ethical Considerations and Challenges

While the potential of AI in healthcare is immense, its deployment raises significant ethical and practical challenges:

- **Data Privacy and Security:** The use of sensitive patient data for AI training and deployment necessitates robust privacy safeguards and compliance with regulations like HIPAA and GDPR.

- **Algorithmic Bias:** Biased training data can lead to AI systems that perform poorly or provide discriminatory recommendations for certain demographic groups, exacerbating health inequalities. Rigorous testing and mitigation strategies are crucial to avoid any kind of bias.
- **Accountability and Liability:** Determining who is responsible when an AI system makes an error that harms a patient (e.g., the developer, the clinician, the hospital) is a complex legal and ethical question.
- **Transparency and Explainability:** The "black box" nature of some AI models can make it difficult for clinicians to understand why a particular recommendation was made, hindering trust and adoption. Explainable AI (XAI) is vital here.
- **Job Displacement:** While AI creates new roles, it may also automate some tasks currently performed by healthcare professionals, raising concerns about workforce transformation.
- **Regulatory Frameworks:** Developing appropriate regulatory frameworks that keep pace with rapid AI advancements while ensuring safety and efficacy is an ongoing challenge for governments worldwide.

Conclusion

Artificial Intelligence is poised to redefine healthcare, pharmaceuticals, and life sciences irrespective of challenges and initial governance issues. By enhancing every stage from fundamental research and drug discovery to personalized treatment and patient management, AI promises to make healthcare more precise, accessible, and efficient. While ethical considerations and regulatory challenges must be carefully navigated, the transformative potential of AI to improve human health and well-being is undeniable. As AI continues to mature, its integration will lead to a healthier, more personalized, and more proactive future for global health.

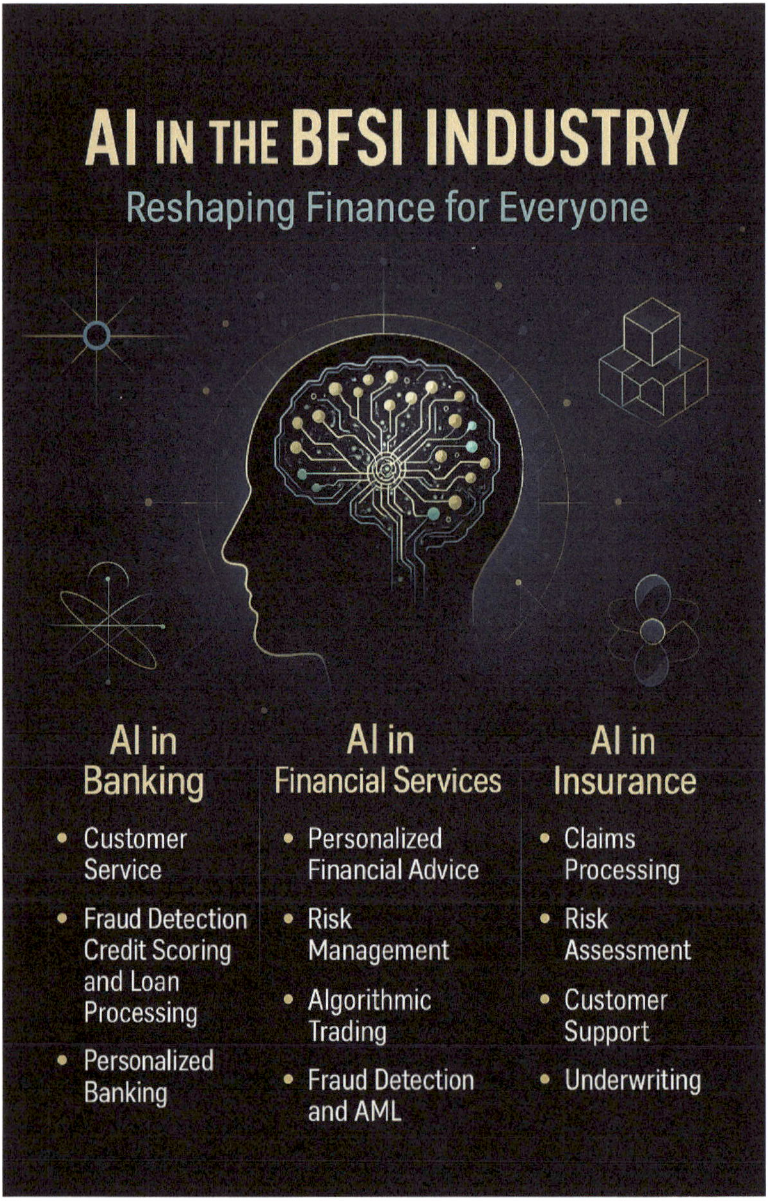
AI IN THE BFSI INDUSTRY
Reshaping Finance for Everyone
AI in Banking
Customer Service
Fraud Detection Credit Scoring and Loan Processing
Personalized Banking
AI in Financial Services
Personalized Financial Advice
Risk Management
Algorithmic Trading
Fraud Detection and AML
AI in Insurance
Claims Processing
Risk Assessment
Customer Support
Underwriting

CHAPTER 9

AI IN THE BFSI INDUSTRY: RESHAPING FINANCE FOR EVERYONE

The Banking, Financial Services, and Insurance (BFSI) industry, a cornerstone of the global economy, is undergoing a profound transformation driven by Artificial Intelligence. From how we manage our money to how institutions assess risk and make investments, AI is introducing unprecedented levels of efficiency, personalization, and security. This chapter explores how AI is revolutionizing various sectors within BFSI, detailing its current applications, the future outlook, and real-world examples, presented in a way that is accessible to both financial experts and everyday consumers.

AI in Banking

Banking, traditionally seen as a conservative industry, is rapidly embracing AI to enhance customer experience, streamline operations, and bolster security. AI driven automation is changing everything from routine transactions to complex financial analysis.

Enhanced Customer Service and Experience

- **AI-powered Chatbots and Virtual Assistants:** Banks are deploying AI chatbots to handle routine customer inquiries, provide instant support, and guide users through transactions 24/7. This improves response times, reduces call center volumes, and enhances customer satisfaction. For instance, Bank of America's (BoA) virtual assistant, Erica, has handled millions of customer inquiries, demonstrating significant efficiency gains. BoA has reported over 98% users get answers they need from Erica.
- **Personalized Financial Advice:** AI analyzes customer spending patterns, financial goals, and risk tolerance to offer personalized product recommendations, investment advice, and budgeting insights. This allows banks to provide tailored services that meet individual customer needs.

Fraud Detection and Security

- **Real-time Transaction Monitoring:** AI algorithms monitor millions of transactions in real-time, identifying anomalous patterns that may indicate fraudulent activity (e.g., unusual spending locations, large transactions, rapid successive purchases). This enables banks to flag and prevent fraud before it occurs, saving billions annually.

- **Anti-Money Laundering (AML) and Know Your Customer (KYC):** AI enhances AML and KYC processes by analyzing vast datasets to detect suspicious financial activities and verify customer identities more efficiently and accurately, reducing false positives and improving compliance.

Credit Scoring and Loan Underwriting

- **Advanced Risk Assessment:** AI models analyze a broader range of data points (beyond traditional credit scores) to assess creditworthiness, including behavioral data and alternative financial data. This allows for more accurate risk assessment, particularly for underserved populations.
- **Automated Loan Processing:** AI automates parts of the loan application and underwriting process, speeding up approvals and reducing operational costs.

Operational Efficiency

- **Robotic Process Automation (RPA):** AI driven RPA automates repetitive, rule-based tasks like data entry, reconciliation, and report generation, freeing up human employees for more complex work.
- **Predictive Analytics for Branch Optimization:** AI analyzes customer traffic and transaction data to optimize branch locations, staffing levels, and service offerings.

Future Outlook in Banking

The future of AI in banking is poised for even greater transformation. We can expect hyper-personalization of financial advice, with AI acting as a personal financial advisor, optimizing budgets, investment portfolios, and debt management for individuals. Generative AI will likely play a significant role in creating customized financial products and marketing content. AI will also continue to enhance cybersecurity measures, making banking even more secure against evolving threats. The emergence of agentic AI will further automate complex financial tasks, leading to more efficient and responsive banking services.

Real-World Examples in Banking

- **JPMorgan Chase:** Uses AI and machine learning for fraud detection, identifying billions of dollars in potential fraud annually. They also leverage AI for contract analysis, significantly reducing the time spent on legal document review.
- **Wells Fargo:** Uses intelligent assistant Fargo handling more than 245million client interactions, it is powered by Googles Dialogflow and also integrated into Fargo mobile app which is multilingual
- **DBS Bank (Singapore):** Has implemented AI across various operations, including customer service, risk management, and personalized financial advice, leading to improved efficiency and customer satisfaction.

AI in Financial Services (Beyond Traditional Banking)

Financial services, a broad category encompassing wealth management, investment advisory, and financial planning, are being reshaped by AI to offer more tailored and accessible solutions.

Investment Management and Trading

- **Algorithmic Trading:** AI-powered algorithms execute trades at high speeds, analyzing vast amounts of market data, news sentiment, and economic indicators to identify profitable trading opportunities. These systems can react to market fluctuations faster than human traders, leading to optimized execution and reduced slippage.
- **Quantitative Research and Analysis:** AI automates the process of analyzing financial data, identifying patterns, and generating insights that inform investment decisions. Machine learning models can predict market movements, identify arbitrage opportunities, and assess the performance of various assets with greater accuracy and speed than traditional methods.
- **Portfolio Management and Robo-Advisors:** AI based robo advisors provide automated, algorithm driven financial planning services with minimal human supervision. They construct and rebalance portfolios based on client risk profiles and financial goals, making investment advice accessible to a wider audience.

Risk Management and Compliance

- **Enhanced Risk Assessment:** AI enhances risk assessment by continuously monitoring market volatility, credit risk, and liquidity risk across complex portfolios. It can identify emerging risks, stress-test portfolios against various scenarios, and provide real-time alerts, allowing institutions to manage exposure more effectively.

- **Fraud Detection and Market Surveillance:** AI systems monitor trading activities for suspicious patterns that could indicate market manipulation, insider trading, or other illicit activities. This helps regulatory bodies and exchanges maintain fair and transparent markets.
- **Automated Compliance:** AI automates the process of ensuring compliance with complex financial regulations. It can monitor communications, transactions, and trading activities to identify potential breaches, reducing the burden of manual compliance checks.

Future Outlook in Financial Services

The future of AI in financial services points towards even more sophisticated predictive analytics, enabling hyper-personalized investment strategies and real-time risk assessments. Generative AI will likely assist in creating complex financial models and reports, while agentic AI could manage entire investment portfolios autonomously, adapting to market changes in real-time. The focus will shift towards proactive financial management and highly customized client experiences.

Real-World Examples in Financial Services

- **BlackRock (Aladdin Platform):** BlackRock's Aladdin is a comprehensive AI-powered platform used by financial institutions globally for risk management, portfolio construction, and trading. It processes vast amounts of data to provide insights into market dynamics and investment performance.

- **Wealthfront & Betterment:** These leading robo-advisors use AI algorithms to manage investment portfolios for millions of clients, offering automated rebalancing, tax-loss harvesting, and personalized financial planning advice.
- **Fidelity Investments:** Utilizes AI and machine learning for various applications, including enhancing customer service through virtual assistants, optimizing investment research, and improving cybersecurity measures.

AI in Insurance

The insurance industry, traditionally reliant on historical data and manual processes, is being transformed by AI to offer more accurate risk assessments, personalized policies, and efficient claims processing.

Underwriting and Pricing

- **Personalized Underwriting and Pricing:** AI analyzes a wider rangc of data points, beyond traditional demographics, such as behavioral data (e.g., driving habits from telematics, health data from wearables) to assess risk more accurately. This allows insurers to offer personalized premiums and policies tailored to individual risk profiles, leading to reasonable pricing and reduced adverse selection.
- **Dynamic Pricing:** AI enables dynamic pricing models that adjust premiums in real-time based on changing risk factors or behavioral data. This is certainly not individuals want, but it is important to know such strategies are going to be used.

Claims Processing

- **Automated Claims Processing:** AI streamlines the claims process by automating initial claim intake, document verification, and even damage assessment (using computer vision for property or vehicle damage). This significantly reduces processing times, minimizes fraudulent claims, and improves customer satisfaction. For example, AI can quickly analyze photos and videos taken by drones to estimate repair costs, with no to minimal human touch points.
- **Fraud Detection:** AI algorithms identify suspicious patterns in claims data that may indicate fraud, such as unusual claim frequency, inconsistent information, or connections between different claimants. This helps insurers prevent significant financial losses due to fraudulent activities.

Customer Engagement and Product Development

- **Enhanced Customer Engagement:** AI powered chatbots and virtual assistants provide instant support for policy inquiries, claims status updates, and general information, offering 24/7 availability and reducing the workload on human agents.
- **Personalized Product Recommendations:** AI analyzes customer data to recommend suitable insurance products and coverage options based on their life stage, needs, and risk profile. For existing customers, it can help upsell additional services.
- **Product Development:** AI analyzes market trends, customer needs, and emerging risks to help insurers design new, innovative insurance products. For instance, AI can identify demand for parametric insurance (triggered by specific events like

extreme weather) or micro insurance tailored to specific lifestyle needs.

Loss Prevention and Risk Management

- **Predictive Analytics:** AI identifies potential risks and helps policyholders take preventive measures. For example, in property insurance, AI can analyze weather patterns and property data to alert homeowners about potential flood risks.
- **IoT Integration:** AI integrates with IoT devices (e.g., smart home sensors) to monitor risks in real-time and offer proactive advice or even trigger automated responses (e.g., shutting off water in case of a leak).

Future Outlook in Insurance

The future of AI in insurance will see even greater personalization of policies, with dynamic pricing models that adjust premiums in real-time based on behavioral data and external factors. Predictive AI will enable proactive risk mitigation, where insurers can offer advice or interventions to prevent claims from occurring. Generative AI will assist in creating highly customized policy documents and marketing materials. Insurance industry will move towards a more preventative and personalized model, driven by continuous AI powered insights.

Real-World Examples in Insurance

- **Lemonade:** This insurtech company uses AI extensively to process claims rapidly, often within seconds, by analyzing claim details and cross-referencing them with policy information and fraud detection algorithms. They also use AI for personalized pricing.

- **Zurich Insurance:** Deploys AI to analyze large datasets, including historical claims, weather patterns, and economic indicators, to improve risk assessment and underwriting accuracy across various lines of business.
- **Metromile:** Utilizes AI and telematics data from car sensors to offer pay-per-mile car insurance, where premiums are based on actual driving behavior, promoting safer driving and reasonable pricing.

AI in Credit Unions (US) or Cooperative Banks (India)

Credit unions, known for their member-centric approach, are leveraging AI to enhance member experience, improve operational efficiency, and compete with larger financial institutions while maintaining their community focus.

Personalized Member Services

- AI helps credit unions understand individual member needs and preferences, enabling them to offer personalized product recommendations, financial advice, and proactive support. This strengthens member relationships and loyalty.

Loan Application Processing

- AI automates parts of the loan application process, from data extraction and verification to initial credit assessments. This speeds up loan approvals, making it easier and faster for members to access funds.

Fraud Detection and Security

- AI systems monitor transactions and member behavior in real-time to detect and prevent fraudulent activities, protecting members' accounts and the credit union's assets. This is particularly crucial for smaller institutions with limited resources.

Operational Efficiency

- AI automates routine administrative tasks such as data entry, compliance checks, and report generation, freeing up staff to focus on more complex member interactions and strategic initiatives. This improves overall productivity and reduces operational costs.

Financial Wellness Tools

- AI powered tools can analyze members' spending habits and financial goals to provide personalized budgeting advice, savings recommendations, and debt management strategies, helping members improve their financial health.

Future Outlook in Credit Unions

AI will enable credit unions to offer hyper-personalized digital banking experiences, matching those of large commercial banks. AI driven insights will allow for more proactive engagement with members, anticipating their needs and offering solutions before they even ask. The future will see AI supporting credit unions and cooperative banks in expanding their reach, offering more sophisticated financial products, and maintaining their competitive edge through enhanced efficiency and member satisfaction.

Real-World Examples in Credit Unions

- **America First Credit Union:** Has implemented AI models across its operations to enhance member lifecycle management, from personalized marketing to fraud detection, demonstrating how AI can be scaled within a credit union environment.
- **Vancity (Canada):** Explores AI for social impact, using data analytics to identify members who might be vulnerable to financial exploitation and offering proactive support, aligning with the credit union's community values.
- **Various Credit Unions using Chatbots:** Many credit unions are deploying AI-powered chatbots on their websites and mobile apps to provide 24/7, member support, answer common questions, and guide members through basic transactions, improving accessibility and service.

AI in Capital Markets

Capital markets, the global marketplace where companies and governments raise long-term funds, are highly complex and data-intensive. AI is revolutionizing this sector by enhancing decision-making, automating trading strategies, and improving risk management.

Increased Efficiency and Speed

One of the most immediate and impactful changes brought by AI in this space is dramatic increases in operational efficiency and speed. AI based systems are automating repetitive, data intensive tasks that previously required significant human efforts. Capital Market clients with large portfolio specifically take advantage of AI based automation.

Enhanced Decision Making

Predictive decision making is the highlight of traditional finance analytics and gurus; they spend a lot of time and energy to provide highly dependable predictions to manage complex financial investments. AI is significantly helping in processing historical data, statistical models and providing deeper insights and more accurate predictions. AI, particularly machine learning and deep learning, can identify non-linear relationships and subtle patterns in vast, diverse datasets that are invisible to conventional methods. This leads to more informed investment decisions, more precise risk assessments, and more effective trading strategies.

Democratization of Investment

The advancements in AI are contributing to the democratization of investment opportunities. Historically, access to sophisticated financial tools, expert advice, and high-return investment strategies was often limited to institutional investors or high net worth individuals. AI platforms and tools are now making these capabilities available to retail investors. Automated investment platforms, user-friendly analytical tools, and AI driven educational resources are lowering the barriers to enabling more individuals to participate effectively in capital markets. This shift can lead to greater financial inclusion and empower a wider range of individuals to manage their wealth more effectively, fostering a more equitable financial ecosystem.

Risk Management and Compliance

- **Algorithmic Bias:** AI models are training on historical data, and if this data reflects existing societal biases, such AI can continue or even amplify such bias. In capital markets, this could lead to unfair lending practices, discriminatory investment recommendations, or biased risk assessments, impacting certain demographics or market segments disproportionately. In order to prevent this, institutions using AI should meticulously curate data before training, enable bias detection techniques and monitor continuously for AI based system recommendation and outputs.
- **Systemic Risk:** Widespread adoption of AI in capital markets introduces new forms of systemic risk. If many institutions rely on similar AI models or data sources, a collective failure or a coordinated market reaction to an AI driven signal could trigger widespread instability. For example, an algorithmic flash crash, where automated trading systems rapidly sell off assets, could be exacerbated by interconnected AI systems. The complexity and speed of AI driven markets make it challenging to identify and mitigate these systemic risks, requiring new regulatory oversight and stress-testing methodologies.

Future Outlook in Capital Markets

The future of AI in capital markets will be characterized by increasingly autonomous trading systems, hyper-personalized investment products, and real-time, predictive risk management. Generative AI will likely play a role in creating sophisticated financial reports and market analyses. The integration of AI with quantum computing could unlock unprecedented capabilities for complex financial modeling and optimization. The market will become even more efficient, data-driven, and responsive, with AI acting as a central nervous system.

Real-World Examples in Capital Markets

- **Goldman Sachs:** Utilizes AI and machine learning for various applications, including optimizing trading strategies, enhancing risk management, and improving client analytics. Their data scientists develop AI models to gain deeper insights into market behavior.
- **Two Sigma:** A prominent hedge fund that relies heavily on AI and machine learning to develop sophisticated quantitative trading strategies. Their AI systems analyze massive datasets to identify subtle market inefficiencies and execute trades.
- **Bloomberg:** Integrates AI into its terminal services, providing financial professionals with AI-powered analytics, sentiment analysis of news, and predictive insights to aid in investment decisions and market monitoring.

Challenges and Ethical Considerations

Despite the immense benefits, the adoption of AI in BFSI faces several challenges and ethical considerations:

- **Data Privacy and Security:** Handling sensitive financial and personal data requires robust cybersecurity measures and strict adherence to data protection regulations (e.g., GDPR, CCPA).
- **Algorithmic Bias:** As mentioned before, AI models trained on biased historical data can perpetuate or even amplify discrimination in credit decisions, insurance pricing, or fraud detection, leading to unfair outcomes for certain demographic groups. Ensuring fairness and explainability is paramount.
- **Regulatory Compliance:** The rapidly evolving nature of AI makes it challenging for regulators to keep pace, leading to a need for agile and adaptive regulatory frameworks.
- **Explainability and Transparency:** The "black box" nature of some complex AI models can make it difficult to explain decisions to customers or regulators, especially in critical areas like loan rejections or insurance claim denials.
- **Job Displacement:** Automation of routine tasks by AI and RPA may lead to job displacement in certain roles within the BFSI sector, necessitating workforce retraining and adaptation strategies.
- **Trust and Adoption:** Building customer trust in AI-driven financial services requires transparency, clear communication, and demonstrable benefits.

Conclusion

Artificial Intelligence is not just a technological enhancement but a fundamental transformation for the BFSI sector. By enabling more accurate risk assessment, personalized customer experiences, efficient operations, and robust fraud detection, AI is driving unprecedented levels of innovation and competitiveness. While navigating the ethical and regulatory complexities is crucial, the continued integration of AI will undoubtedly lead to a more secure, efficient, and customer-centric financial future. The BFSI industry is at the forefront of leveraging AI to redefine how financial services are delivered and consumed globally.

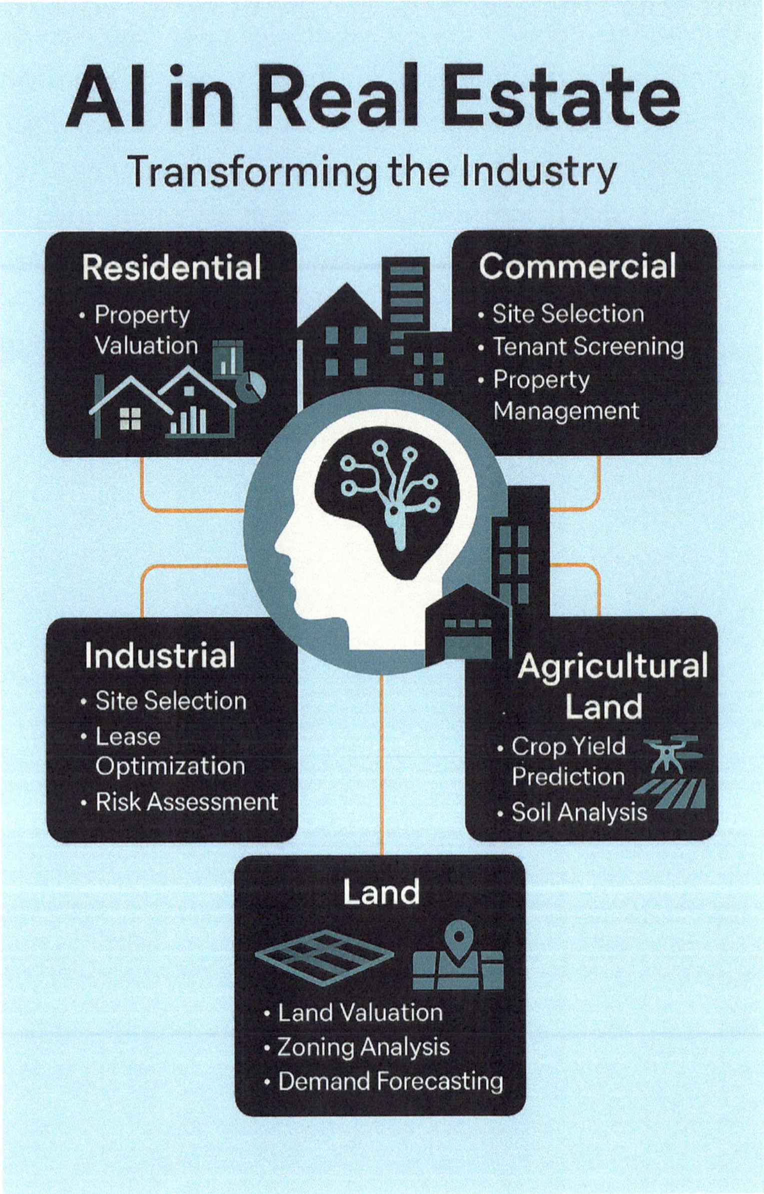
AI in Real Estate
Transforming the Industry
Residential
• Property Valuation
Commercial
• Site Selection
• Tenant Screening
• Property Management
Industrial
• Site Selection
• Lease Optimization
• Risk Assessment
Agricultural Land
• Crop Yield Prediction
• Soil Analysis
Land
• Land Valuation
• Zoning Analysis
• Demand Forecasting

CHAPTER 10

AI IN REAL ESTATE

Artificial Intelligence is rapidly transforming the real estate industry, moving beyond traditional practices to introduce unprecedented levels of efficiency, insight, and personalization. From how properties are valued and managed to how new developments are planned and executed, AI is becoming an indispensable tool for professionals and a significant factor for individuals navigating the housing market. This chapter explores significant impact of AI across various real estate sectors, demonstrating its role in driving innovation and creating a more efficient real estate industry.

AI in Residential Real Estate

Residential real estate, encompassing single-family homes (SFR) and multi-family dwellings, is where many individuals first encounter AI's influence in the property market. AI is enhancing every stage of the residential property lifecycle, from search and valuation to management and investment.

Single-Family Residential (SFR)

For individual homeowners and buyers, AI is making the process of finding, buying, and selling homes more efficient and transparent. AI-powered platforms analyze vast datasets, including property characteristics, historical sales data, neighborhood demographics, and even local amenities, to provide highly accurate property valuations. This moves beyond simple comparative market analyses, incorporating predictive analytics to forecast future property values based on market trends and economic indicators. For sellers, AI can optimize listing prices and identify the best times to list properties. For buyers, AI-driven search engines can filter properties based on highly specific preferences, learning from user interactions to refine recommendations and even suggest properties that users might not have initially considered but align with their lifestyle.

AI also plays a crucial role in property management for SFRs. Predictive maintenance algorithms analyze data from smart home devices to anticipate potential issues with appliances or structural components, allowing for proactive repairs before costly breakdowns occur. This not only saves homeowners money but also enhances the living experience. Virtual staging, powered by generative AI, allows potential buyers to visualize empty homes with different furniture and decor styles, making listings more appealing and reducing the need for physical staging.

Beyond these applications, AI is increasingly vital in the financial aspects of SFRs:

- **Underwriting:** AI streamlines the underwriting process by rapidly analyzing vast amounts of borrower data, credit histories, property characteristics, and market conditions. This leads to faster loan approvals, more accurate risk assessments, and reduced manual errors, benefiting both lenders and borrowers.

AI can identify patterns indicative of default risk that might be missed by human underwriters, leading to more robust lending decisions.

- **Investments:** AI empowers SFR investors by identifying lucrative investment opportunities. It analyzes market trends, demographic shifts, rental demand, and property performance data to pinpoint undervalued assets or emerging growth areas. AI driven platforms can forecast potential returns, assess risk profiles of individual properties or portfolios, and even suggest optimal acquisition strategies, allowing investors to make data-backed decisions with greater confidence.
- **Portfolio Management:** For investors with multiple SFR properties, AI provides comprehensive tools for portfolio optimization. It monitors the performance of each asset, tracks key metrics like occupancy rates, rental income, and maintenance costs, and identifies underperforming properties. AI can recommend strategies for rent adjustments, property improvements, or divestment to maximize overall portfolio returns and minimize vacancies.
- **Asset Management:** AI enhances the day-to-day management of SFR assets. This includes predictive maintenance scheduling, optimizing vendor selection for repairs, and automating communication with tenants regarding rent payments or service requests. AI tools can analyze tenant behavior and preferences to improve retention rates and ensure a positive living experience, ultimately preserving asset value.
- **Debt Management:** AI assists in optimizing debt structures for SFR portfolios. It can analyze interest rate trends, market

liquidity, and property cash flows to recommend optimal refinancing opportunities or debt restructuring strategies. AI driven financial models help investors manage their debt obligations efficiently, minimizing interest expenses and maximizing equity growth.

Multi-Family Residential

In the multi-family sector (Apartments, Condominiums and Town Homes), AI is revolutionizing property management, tenant relations, and investment strategies. AI based systems streamline leasing processes by automating lead qualification, scheduling tours, and even generating lease agreements. Chatbots and virtual assistants provide 24/7 support to prospective and current tenants, answering frequently asked questions, processing maintenance requests, and fostering a sense of responsiveness.

For property managers, AI optimizes operational efficiency. Predictive analytics can forecast tenant turnover, allowing managers to proactively market vacant units and minimize loss of income. AI also enhances energy management by optimizing HVAC systems and lighting based on occupancy patterns and external weather conditions, leading to significant cost savings and reduced environmental impact. In terms of security, AI powered surveillance systems can detect unusual activity and alert management to potential threats, enhancing safety for residents. Investors in multi-family properties leverage AI for more sophisticated market analysis, identifying emerging neighborhoods, predicting rental demand, and assessing the financial viability of potential acquisitions with greater accuracy.

In addition to these operational benefits, AI significantly impacts the financial and strategic aspects of multi-family real estate:

- **Underwriting:** AI streamlines the underwriting process for multi-family properties. It can quickly process and analyze complex financial statements, rent rolls, operating expenses, and market comparables. By identifying delicate correlations and risk factors, AI provides a more nuanced assessment of a property's financial viability and potential returns, leading to more informed and efficient deal closures.
- **Investments:** AI empowers multi-family investors to identify optimal investment opportunities by analyzing vast datasets, including demographic trends, employment growth, rental market dynamics, and historical performance. AI driven models can predict future rental growth, vacancy rates, and property appreciation, enabling investors to pinpoint high-potential assets and construct diversified portfolios that align with their risk appetite and return objectives.
- **Portfolio Management:** For large multi-family portfolios, AI offers advanced analytics to monitor and optimize performance across all assets. It provides real-time insights into property-level performance, identifies underperforming assets, and suggests strategic interventions such as rent adjustments, capital improvements, or disposition strategies to maximize overall portfolio value and yield. AI can also model various market scenarios to stress-test portfolio resilience.
- **Asset Management:** AI enhances the operational efficiency and value preservation of multi-family assets. This includes

optimizing pricing strategies for units based on demand and competitor analysis, automating maintenance scheduling through predictive analytics, and improving tenant satisfaction through personalized communication and proactive issue resolution. AI tools can also monitor energy consumption and recommend adjustments to reduce operating costs and improve sustainability.

- **Debt Management:** AI plays a crucial role in optimizing the debt structures of multi-family properties. It analyzes interest rate forecasts, loan covenants, and property cash flows to identify opportune moments for refinancing, debt restructuring, or securing new financing at favorable terms. AI driven financial modeling helps property owners and investors manage their debt obligations strategically, minimizing financial risk and enhancing profitability.

AI in Commercial Real Estate

Commercial real estate (CRE) is a diverse sector where AI is driving significant innovation across various property types, from office buildings to specialized facilities.

Office Buildings

AI is transforming office spaces into smart, efficient, and responsive environments. AI-powered building management systems optimize energy consumption, lighting, and climate control based on occupancy patterns, external weather, and even individual preferences, reducing operational costs and carbon footprint. Predictive maintenance algorithms analyze data from building sensors to anticipate equipment failures (e.g., HVAC, elevators) before they occur, minimizing downtime and maintenance costs. For tenants, AI enhances the workplace experience through smart access control, personalized environmental settings, and intelligent space utilization tools that help optimize office layouts and meeting room bookings. AI also assists in lease management, providing insights into tenant behavior and optimizing lease terms.

Retail Properties

In the retail sector, AI is helping property owners and managers adapt to evolving consumer behaviors and the rise of e-commerce. AI based analytics can assess foot traffic patterns, optimize store layouts, and personalize marketing efforts to attract and retain shoppers. By analyzing sales data, demographic information, and social media trends, AI can predict consumer demand for certain products or services, informing tenant mix strategies and ensuring a vibrant retail environment. AI also supports security and loss prevention through intelligent surveillance systems that can detect suspicious activities. For shopping centers, AI can optimize parking management and provide personalized navigation within the complex, enhancing the overall customer experience.

Hotels and Hospitality

AI is revolutionizing the hospitality industry by enhancing guest experiences, optimizing operations, and improving revenue management. AI powered chatbots and virtual concierges provide instant customer service, handling bookings, answering queries, and fulfilling requests 24/7. Predictive analytics enable hotels to forecast occupancy rates, optimize pricing strategies, and personalize offers based on guest preferences and historical data, boosting revenue potential. AI also streamlines back office operations, from optimizing housekeeping schedules to managing inventory and supply chains. Smart room technologies, integrated with AI, allow guests to control lighting, temperature, and entertainment systems with voice commands, creating a seamless and personalized stay. AI driven sentiment analysis of guest reviews provides actionable insights for continuous service improvement.

Mixed-Use Developments

Mixed-use properties, which combine residential, commercial, retail, and sometimes hospitality spaces, present unique management challenges and opportunities. AI is crucial for integrating and optimizing the diverse functions within these complex developments. AI platforms can manage shared resources, such as parking and security, across different property types, ensuring efficient operation. Predictive analytics can balance the needs of various tenants and residents, optimizing traffic flow, energy usage, and amenity scheduling. AI also facilitates a cohesive community experience by personalizing services and communications for different user groups within the development, fostering engagement and satisfaction.

Special Purpose Properties (e.g., Self-Storage)

Even specialized commercial properties like self-storage facilities are benefiting from AI. AI-driven systems can automate many aspects of self-storage management, including online bookings, access control, and billing. Predictive analytics can forecast demand for storage units, optimize pricing, and identify units likely to become vacant, allowing for proactive marketing. AI based surveillance systems enhance security by monitoring premises and alerting staff to unusual activity. Chatbots can handle customer inquiries, provide facility information, and assist with rental processes, improving customer service and reducing the need for constant human oversight.

AI in Industrial Real Estate

Industrial real estate, encompassing warehouses, manufacturing facilities, data centers, and heavy manufacturing plants, its a sector where AI's impact on operational efficiency, logistics, and automation is particularly profound.

Warehouses

AI is at the heart of the modern, automated warehouse. AI powered robotics and autonomous guided vehicles (AGVs) handle tasks like picking, packing, and sorting, significantly increasing speed and accuracy while reducing labor costs. Predictive analytics optimize inventory management, forecasting demand and ensuring optimal stock levels to prevent overstocking or shortages. AI-driven route optimization algorithms improve the efficiency of goods movement within the warehouse and for last-mile delivery, reducing fuel consumption and delivery times. Computer vision systems enhance quality control by inspecting goods for defects and ensuring proper packaging. AI also plays a role in warehouse safety by monitoring equipment and human activity to prevent accidents.

Manufacturing Facilities

In manufacturing, AI is enabling the transition to smart factories and advanced production processes. Predictive maintenance, powered by AI, monitors machinery in real-time, identifying potential failures before they occur, thereby minimizing downtime and extending equipment lifespan. AI driven quality control systems use computer vision to inspect products at various stages of production, ensuring high standards and reducing waste. AI also optimizes production schedules, manages supply chains, and improves energy efficiency within facilities. Robotics, often guided by AI, perform repetitive or dangerous tasks, enhancing safety and precision. The integration of AI allows for greater flexibility and responsiveness in manufacturing, enabling rapid adaptation to changing market demands.

Data Centers

Data centers are the backbone of the digital economy, and their efficiency is paramount. AI is critical for optimizing data center operations, particularly in managing energy consumption and cooling. AI powered systems monitor server performance, temperature, and humidity, dynamically adjusting cooling systems and power distribution to maximize efficiency and minimize energy waste. Predictive analytics can anticipate hardware failures, allowing for proactive maintenance and preventing costly outages. AI also enhances security within data centers through intelligent surveillance and access control systems. Given the massive energy footprint of data centers, AI's ability to optimize their operations has significant environmental and economic benefits.

Heavy Manufacturing

In heavy manufacturing industries, such as automotive, aerospace, and construction, AI is improving safety, efficiency, and quality control. AI powered robotics can handle large, heavy, or hazardous materials, reducing the risk of human injury. Computer vision systems inspect structural components, and finished products for defects with high precision. Predictive analytics optimize the maintenance of large-scale machinery, preventing costly breakdowns and ensuring continuous operation. AI also assists in complex design and simulation processes, allowing engineers to test and refine products virtually before going for physical production, leading to more robust and efficient designs. The integration of AI in heavy manufacturing contributes to safer working environments, higher quality products, and more streamlined production lines.

AI in Land and Agricultural Real Estate

AI is also making significant inroads into the land and agricultural real estate sectors, transforming how land is managed, developed, and utilized for food production.

Undeveloped Land

For undeveloped land, AI provides powerful tools for assessment and planning. AI powered geospatial analysis can evaluate land suitability for various purposes (e.g., residential, commercial, conservation) by analyzing factors like topography, soil composition, water access, and environmental regulations. This helps developers and investors make more informed decisions about land acquisition and potential uses. AI can also predict future land value appreciation based on urban growth patterns, infrastructure development plans, and demographic shifts, offering valuable insights for long-term investment strategies. Furthermore, AI can assist in identifying environmental risks or opportunities, such as potential for renewable energy installations or ecological restoration.

Land Designed for Future Development

For land earmarked for future development, AI streamlines the planning and design process. Generative AI can create optimized master plans for communities, considering factors like traffic flow, green spaces, utility infrastructure, and aesthetic appeal. AI driven simulations can model the impact of proposed developments on local ecosystems, traffic, and public services, allowing planners to mitigate potential negative consequences. AI also assists in regulatory compliance by analyzing zoning laws and building codes, ensuring that development plans adhere to all necessary requirements. This leads to more efficient, sustainable, and community-friendly urban planning.

Agricultural Real Estate

In agricultural real estate, AI is at the forefront of precision agriculture, maximizing yields while minimizing environmental impact. AI powered drones and sensors collect data on crop health, soil conditions, and weather patterns. AI algorithms then analyze this data to provide precise recommendations for irrigation, fertilization, and pest control, reducing waste and optimizing resource use. Predictive analytics can forecast crop yields and detect early signs of disease or pest infestations, allowing farmers to take timely action. AI also assists in managing livestock, monitoring animal health, and optimizing feeding schedules. For agricultural investors, AI can assess the productivity and profitability of farmland, identify optimal crop rotations, and predict market prices for agricultural commodities, leading to more informed investment decisions.

AI in Property Valuation and Investment

Accurate property valuation and data driven investment decisions are critical in real estate. AI is revolutionizing these areas by leveraging vast datasets and advanced algorithms:

- **Automated Valuation Models (AVMs):** AI powered AVMs analyze numerous data points, including property characteristics (size, number of rooms, age), location (school districts, crime rates, proximity to amenities), market trends, comparable sales, and even satellite imagery or street view data. This allows for rapid, accurate, and objective property valuations, significantly reducing the time and cost associated with traditional appraisals.
- **Predictive Market Analysis:** AI algorithms can forecast future property values, rental yields, and market trends by analyzing historical data, economic indicators, demographic shifts,

infrastructure development plans, and even social media sentiment. This enables investors to identify emerging opportunities and risks, making more strategic decisions.

- **Investment Opportunity Identification:** AI can sift through vast databases of properties to identify those that meet specific investment criteria (e.g., high rental yield, potential for appreciation, distressed assets), streamlining the due diligence process for investors.
- **Risk Assessment:** AI assesses various risks associated with real estate investments, such as market volatility, tenant default risk, and environmental factors, providing a more comprehensive risk profile.

AI in Property Search and Recommendation

For buyers and renters, the property search process can be overwhelming. AI is personalizing and streamlining this experience:

- **Personalized Property Recommendations:** AI analyzes user preferences, search history, browsing behavior, and even lifestyle data to provide highly tailored property recommendations. Beyond basic filters, AI can understand nuanced preferences like "a quiet neighborhood with good schools" or "a vibrant area with nightlife."
- **Natural Language Search:** AI based search interfaces allow users to describe their ideal property in natural language (e.g., "Find me a 3-bedroom house with a big yard in a family-friendly area near downtown"), making the search process more intuitive and efficient.

- **Virtual Property Tours and Chatbots:** AI driven virtual tours (often combined with VR/AR) allow prospective buyers to explore properties remotely. AI chatbots can answer common questions about listings, schedule viewings, and provide instant information 24/7, enhancing customer engagement.
- **Sentiment Analysis of Neighborhoods:** AI can analyze online reviews, social media discussions, and news articles to gauge public sentiment about specific neighborhoods, providing insights into community dynamics, safety, and quality of life.

AI in Property Management and Operations

AI is optimizing various aspects of property management, leading to increased efficiency and cost savings for landlords and property managers:

- **Predictive Maintenance:** AI analyzes data from IoT sensors (e.g., HVAC systems, plumbing, electrical) to predict equipment failures before they occur, enabling proactive maintenance. This reduces repair costs, minimizes downtime for tenants, and extends the lifespan of assets.
- **Tenant Management and Support:** AI-powered platforms can automate tenant communication, handle maintenance requests, process rent payments, and provide instant support for common issues, improving tenant satisfaction and reducing administrative workload.
- **Energy Optimization:** AI systems can optimize energy consumption in commercial and residential buildings by analyzing usage patterns, weather data, and occupancy levels, leading to significant utility cost savings and improved sustainability.

- **Security and Surveillance:** AI powered security systems use computer vision for facial recognition, pet monitoring, anomaly detection, and access control, enhancing safety and security in properties.
- **Lease Management and Compliance:** AI automates the drafting, review, and management of lease agreements, ensuring compliance with legal requirements and tracking key dates and clauses.

AI in Construction and Development

AI is also making inroads into the construction areas of real estate, improving project management, safety, and design:

- **Project Management and Scheduling:** AI optimizes construction schedules, predicts potential delays, and allocates resources efficiently by analyzing project data, weather forecasts, and supply chain information.
- **Safety Monitoring:** AI-powered computer vision systems can monitor construction sites for safety hazards, detect non-compliance with safety protocols, and identify workers not wearing proper protective equipment, reducing accidents.
- **Generative Design:** AI can generate multiple design options for buildings or spaces based on specified parameters (e.g., budget, materials, functionality, environmental factors), helping architects and developers explore innovative and optimized designs.
- **Quality Control:** AI based drones and cameras can inspect construction progress and identify defects or deviations from design plans, ensuring higher quality builds.

Challenges and Future Outlook

Despite its transformative potential, AI adoption in real estate faces challenges:

- **Data Availability and Quality:** The real estate industry is often fragmented, and access to comprehensive, standardized, and high-quality data can be a significant hurdle.
- **Integration with Legacy Systems:** Many real estate companies rely on outdated legacy systems, making AI integration complex and costly.
- **Talent Gap:** A shortage of AI-savvy professionals within the real estate sector can hinder adoption and effective implementation.
- **Ethical Concerns:** Issues around data privacy, algorithmic bias in property recommendations or valuations, and job displacement require careful consideration and robust ethical frameworks.

However, the future of AI in real estate is bright. As data becomes more accessible and AI technologies mature, we can expect:

- **Increased Automation:** More routine tasks will be automated, allowing professionals to focus on strategic and innovation-based work activities.
- **Hyper-Personalization:** Property experiences will become even more tailored to individual needs and preferences.
- **Smart Cities Integration:** AI in real estate will increasingly integrate with broader smart city initiatives, optimizing urban living.

- **Sustainability Focus:** AI will play a larger role in designing, building, and managing energy-efficient and environmentally friendly properties.

Conclusion

AI's pervasive influence across residential, commercial, industrial, and land/agricultural real estate sectors is undeniable. It is transforming how properties are valued, managed, developed, and transacted, bringing unprecedented levels of data-driven insight, efficiency, and automation. For real estate professionals, AI offers powerful tools to enhance decision-making, streamline operations, and identify new opportunities. For common man, it promises more transparent property markets, smarter homes, and more sustainable communities. As AI continues to evolve, its integration with the real estate industry will only deepen, leading to a more intelligent, responsive, and sustainable real estate industry for all stakeholders.

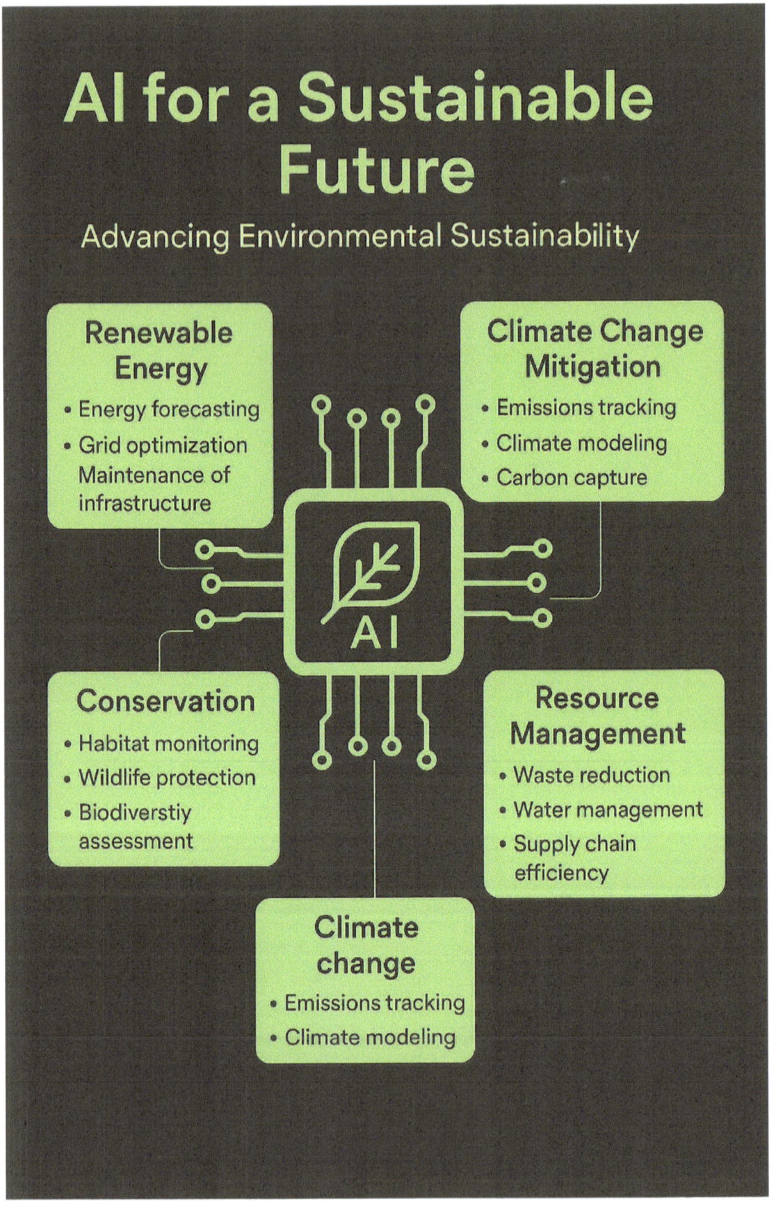
AI for a Sustainable Future
Advancing Environmental Sustainability
Renewable Energy
• Energy forecasting
• Grid optimization
Maintenance of infrastructure
Climate Change Mitigation
• Emissions tracking
• Climate modeling
• Carbon capture
AI
Conservation
• Habitat monitoring
• Wildlife protection
• Biodiverstiy assessment
Resource Management
• Waste reduction
• Water management
• Supply chain efficiency
Climate change
• Emissions tracking
• Climate modeling

CHAPTER 11

AI FOR SUSTAINABLE FUTURE

In an era defined by pressing environmental challenges, Artificial Intelligence is emerging as a powerful ally in the global quest for sustainability. Climate change, biodiversity loss, resource scarcity, and unsustainable development practices threaten not only ecosystems but also economies, health, and human well-being. The urgency to transition toward a more sustainable and resilient planet has never been greater.

Amid this global challenge, AI is proving to be a transformative enabler of environmental sustainability. From predicting climate events to optimizing energy consumption and managing natural resources, AI is providing the tools to balance economic growth with ecological responsibility. This chapter explores various ways AI is empowering environmental conservation and sustainable development, presenting insights that are both accessible to the general reader and valuable for environmental professionals.

The Urgent Need for Sustainable Solutions

The planet faces unprecedented environmental pressures. Traditional approaches to addressing these issues often struggle with the scale and complexity of the problems. This is where AI, with its capacity to process vast datasets, identify intricate patterns, and make predictive analyses, offers a transformative advantage. AI can help us understand environmental systems more deeply, predict future trends, and implement more effective interventions.

Sustainability isn't just about the environment. It's about creating systems, economic, ecological, and way of living that are viable for generations. AI helps operationalize this vision through:

- **Data-driven decision-making:** AI processes vast amounts of environmental data to provide actionable insights.
- **Automation:** AI automates climate change monitoring, analysis, and even intervention processes required. Increasing efficiency and faster actions for climate change with reduced errors.
- **Prediction and modeling:** AI creates sophisticated models to forecast environmental changes and the impact of various interventions. Leading the climate change organizations to be more confident and prepared with short term and long-term solutions.

AI in Environmental Conservation

AI is revolutionizing how we monitor, protect, and manage natural ecosystems and species. Its applications range from tracking wildlife to combating illegal activities and restoring degraded habitats.

Biodiversity Protection

Protecting the Earth's rich biodiversity is crucial for ecological balance and human well-being. AI provides advanced tools for monitoring species, understanding their habitats, and identifying threats.

- **Wildlife Monitoring and Tracking:** AI powered camera traps and drone imagery, combined with computer vision algorithms, can automatically identify and count animal species, track their movements, and monitor population health. This reduces the need for manual, labor-intensive surveys and provides real-time data for conservationists. For instance, AI systems can differentiate individual animals by their unique markings, aiding in population studies of endangered species like tigers or whales.

Real-world examples include wildbook.org, which identifies animals using computer vision, and Rainforest Connection, which detects illegal logging via acoustic sensors.

- **Poaching Prevention:** AI can analyze patterns in sensor data (e.g., from acoustic sensors or satellite imagery) to detect suspicious activities in protected areas, alerting rangers to potential poaching incidents. Predictive models can also identify high-risk areas for poaching, allowing for proactive deployment of resources.

Technologies like SPARROW, an AI-powered edge computing solution, are designed to operate autonomously in remote areas to measure and protect biodiversity.

Another example, AI systems like PAWS (Protection Assistant for Wildlife Security) use predictive analytics to deploy anti-poaching patrols more effectively.

- **Habitat Restoration and Management:** AI can analyze satellite imagery and environmental data to identify areas in need of restoration, monitor the success of restoration efforts, and optimize planting strategies for reforestation or wetland recovery. Machine learning models can predict the most suitable species for a given area based on soil conditions, climate, and other ecological factors.
- **Species Identification and Tracking:** AI driven computer vision can identify individual animals from images or videos, track their patterns, movements, and monitor their health, aiding conservation research and management.
- **Biodiversity Hotspot Identification:** AI can analyze environmental data to identify areas with high biodiversity that are under threat, guiding conservation priorities and resource allocation.

Climate Change Mitigation and Adaptation

AI is a critical tool in the fight against climate change, offering solutions for reducing greenhouse gas emissions and adapting to the impacts of a warming planet.

- **Optimizing Energy Systems:** AI can optimize energy grids by predicting energy demand and supply, integrating renewable energy sources more efficiently, and managing energy storage. This leads to reduced reliance on fossil fuels and a more stable, sustainable energy infrastructure. For example, AI can forecast wind and solar power generation with high accuracy, allowing grid operators to balance the load effectively. Smart Grids use AI to balance real-time energy demands and manage predictive maintenance for renewable energy sources.

- **Smart Agriculture:** As discussed in previous chapter, AI based precision agriculture uses sensors, drones, and satellite data to monitor crop health, soil conditions, and water usage. AI algorithms can then optimize irrigation, fertilization, and pest control, leading to increased yields with reduced resource consumption and lower greenhouse gas emissions from agricultural practices. This also contributes to food security.

Examples include Descartes Labs monitoring crop health via satellite AI, and CropX and Arable optimizing smart irrigation.

- **Carbon Capture and Sequestration:** AI can accelerate the development and optimization of carbon capture technologies by simulating molecular interactions and identifying efficient materials for CO2 absorption. It can also monitor underground CO2 storage sites for leaks, ensuring long-term effectiveness.
- **Climate Modeling and Prediction:** AI enhances the accuracy and speed of climate models, allowing scientists to better understand complex climate systems, predict extreme weather events, and measure the impacts of climate change on various regions. This information is vital for developing effective adaptation strategies and early warning systems. IBM's "Environmental Intelligence" Suite uses AI to detect wildfire risks, and Google Flood Hub predicts floods using AI models.

AI in Sustainable Development

Beyond direct environmental conservation, AI contributes to broader sustainable development goals by improving resource efficiency, fostering circular economies, and enhancing urban sustainability.

Resource Management and Efficiency

AI helps optimize the use of finite resources, reducing waste and promoting more sustainable consumption patterns.

- **Waste Management and Recycling:** AI enabled sorting robots can identify and separate different types of waste materials with high accuracy, improving recycling rates and reducing landfill waste. AI can also optimize waste collection routes, reducing fuel consumption and emissions. Example: AMP Robotics enables automated waste sorting solutions which uses AI
- **Water Management:** AI systems can monitor water quality, detect leaks in water distribution networks, and optimize irrigation schedules in agriculture, leading to significant water savings. Predictive models can forecast water availability, aiding in drought management and resource allocation. Singapore uses AI for urban water conservation.
- **Supply Chain Optimization:** AI can optimize supply chains to reduce their environmental footprint by minimizing transportation distances, reducing spoilage, and improving inventory management. This leads to lower energy consumption and fewer emissions.

Urban Sustainability

AI plays a crucial role in creating smarter, more sustainable cities.

- **Smart Grids and Buildings:** AI optimizes energy consumption in buildings by adjusting heating, ventilation, and air conditioning (HVAC) systems based on occupancy, weather forecasts, and energy prices. Smart grids use AI to manage energy flow, integrate renewables, and prevent blackouts. BrainBoxAI.com reduces HVAC usage in buildings, claiming to reduce 40% reduction in carbon emissions.
- **Traffic Management:** AI-powered systems can optimize traffic flow, reduce congestion, and minimize idling times, leading to lower vehicle emissions and improved air quality. This includes intelligent traffic lights, dynamic routing, and public transportation optimization. Barcelona and Bengaluru use AI for traffic light optimization.
- **Pollution Monitoring and Control:** AI analyzes data from air and water quality sensors to identify pollution sources, predict pollution events, and recommend mitigation strategies. This helps urban planners and policymakers make informed decisions to improve public health and environmental quality. AI uses sensor/weather data for air quality monitoring and pollution mapping.

AI for Environmental Policy and ESG

AI is also enabling better environmental governance and enhancing transparency in Environmental, Social, and Governance (ESG) reporting.

- **Carbon Emissions Tracking:** AI tools can track carbon emissions in real-time across supply chains and operations, providing accurate data for reporting and reduction strategies. Watershed.com tracks near real-time carbon emissions by aggregating data from various sources.
- **ESG Investing Insights:** AI helps investors analyze vast amounts of data to measure companies ESG performance, identify risks, and uncover opportunities for sustainable investments. ESG investors use AI for sentiment and compliance scoring.
- **Policy Making:** Governments use AI to evaluate climate risk, model the impact of environmental policies, and make data-driven decisions for sustainable development.

Challenges and Ethical Considerations

While the potential of AI for sustainability is immense, it's crucial to approach its implementation with realism and address inherent challenges:

- **Data Bias:** AI models are only as good as the data they are trained on. Biased or incomplete environmental data can lead to flawed predictions and ineffective solutions.
- **Energy Consumption of AI:** The training and deployment of large AI models require significant computational resources and energy, contributing to carbon emissions. Developing energy-efficient AI algorithms and infrastructure is critical.
- **Accessibility in Low-Resource Regions:** Ensuring that AI tools and their benefits are accessible to developing nations

and communities with limited resources is essential for equitable sustainable development.

- **Regulatory Frameworks:** Developing policies and regulations that encourage responsible AI innovation for sustainability while mitigating risks is an ongoing challenge. Building a balance and providing equitable guardrails will be crucial.

The Road Ahead: AI + Planetary Health

The future of AI in sustainability points towards even more integrated and proactive solutions. Future applications include:

- **Collaborative AI platforms:** Platforms that facilitate data sharing and collaboration among researchers, policymakers, and communities across various countries.
- **Environmental education through AI tools:** Interactive AI tools that can educate the public about environmental issues and sustainable practices.
- **AI-guided regenerative development:** AI systems that can guide efforts to restore ecosystems and create regenerative economic models.

Conclusion

AI is not a silver bullet. but it is a powerful lever in building a sustainable future. Its ability to analyze complex data, optimize systems, predict trends, and automate processes offers unprecedented opportunities to address climate change, protect biodiversity, foster circular economies, and build more sustainable cities and food systems. While challenges related to data, energy consumption, and ethics must be carefully managed, the strategic application of AI holds the key to accelerating our transition towards a more environmentally responsible, resource-efficient, and equitable world. Embracing AI for sustainability is not just an option but a necessity in our collective journey towards a thriving planet.

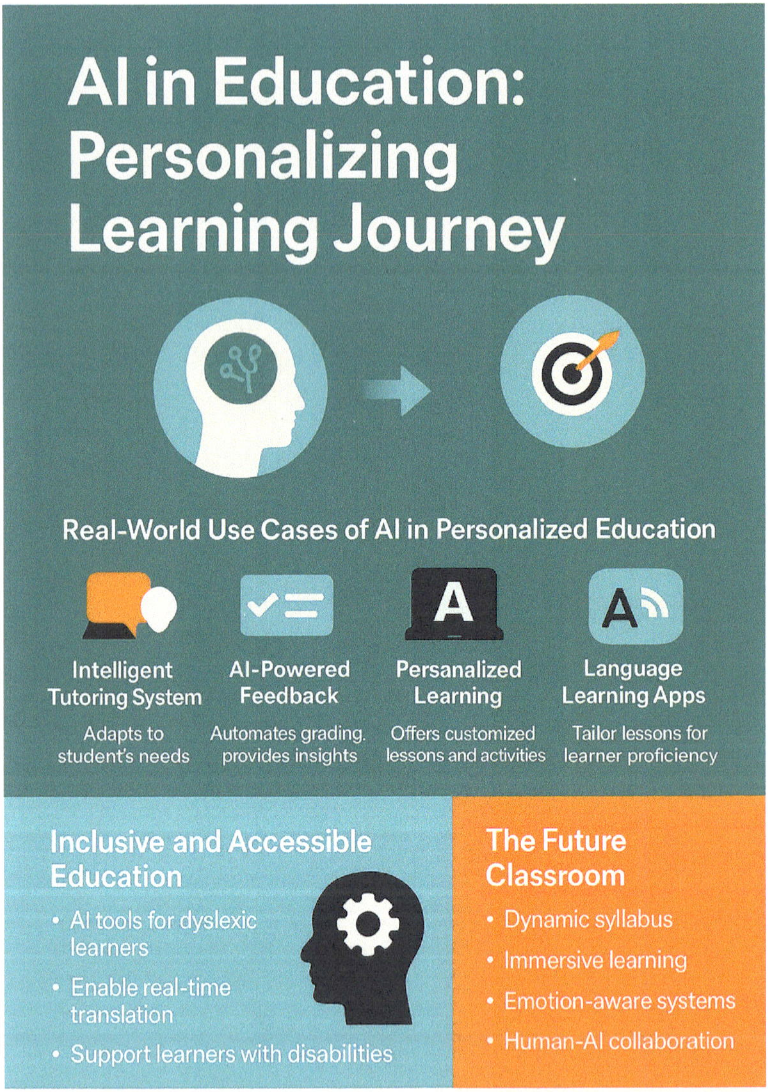

AI Democratizes Learning and Unlocks Human Potential

CHAPTER 12

AI IN EDUCATION: PERSONALIZING THE LEARNING JOURNEY

Artificial Intelligence is poised to revolutionize education, moving beyond traditional one-size-fits-all models to create highly personalized, adaptive, and engaging learning experiences. As classrooms evolve and learning environments diversify from K-12 schools to universities, vocational institutions, and online platforms AI is enabling learning experiences that are highly personalized, inspiring, and inclusive. This chapter explores how AI is reshaping education at every level and for every learner, offering a vision that is both grounded in present innovations and inspired by future possibilities. The integration of AI in education is not merely about technological advancement; it's about fostering a learning environment that nurtures individual potential, addresses diverse needs, and prepares future generations for a rapidly evolving world.

AI in Primary and Secondary Education

AI is enhancing early education by offering personalized tutoring, adaptive learning platforms, and predictive analytics to identify at-risk students. Tools like Carnegie Learning and Squirrel AI use intelligent tutoring systems that adapt to a student's learning pace, cognitive patterns, and subject comprehension. These systems analyze student performance in real-time, identifying areas of struggle and providing targeted interventions, such as supplementary materials, different problem sets, or even suggesting a change in teaching methodology. Natural Language Processing (NLP) enables automated grading and feedback, not just for multiple-choice questions but also for essays and open-ended responses, freeing teachers to focus on creative engagement, individualized mentorship, and addressing the socio-emotional needs of their students. Furthermore, AI can help in curriculum development by identifying gaps in learning materials and suggesting improvements based on student performance data across a cohort.

AI in Higher Education and Universities

Universities are integrating AI to streamline administrative workflows and enhance student engagement. Platforms like Georgia State University's chatbot 'Pounce' guide students through enrollment, financial aid, and course registration, significantly reducing dropout rates by providing instant, accessible support.

AI-powered analytics identify students who may be struggling academically or facing personal challenges, recommending timely academic interventions, counseling services, or peer support. Tools like Gradescope automate grading at scale for quantitative disciplines, allowing instructors to provide more consistent and rapid feedback. Beyond administration, AI is revolutionizing personalized learning paths, helping students align coursework with evolving career goals and industry demands. This includes AI driven career counseling that analyzes market trends and student aptitudes to suggest optimal academic and professional trajectories.

Personalized Learning with AI

Traditional education often struggles to cater to the diverse needs of individual learners. AI addresses this by enabling truly personalized learning pathways, adapting content, pace, and methodology to optimize outcomes for every student.

- **Adaptive Learning Platforms:** As mentioned in chapter 3, AI Powered platforms continuously assess a student's knowledge, strengths, weaknesses, and learning style. They then dynamically adjust the curriculum, provide targeted exercises, and offer resources that match the student's current understanding and preferred learning approach. This ensures that students are neither bored by overly simple material nor overwhelmed by highly complex concepts.
- **Intelligent Tutoring Systems (ITS):** ITS go beyond simple question-and-answer systems. They act as virtual tutors, providing real-time, one-on-one support. They can explain concepts in multiple ways, offer hints, identify misconceptions, and guide students through problem-solving processes, much like a human tutor would. This personalized guidance can significantly improve comprehension and retention.
- **Personalized Content Curation:** AI can curate educational content (articles, videos, simulations, interactive exercises)

from vast online repositories based on a student's learning goals, interests, and past performance. This ensures that learners are always presented with relevant and engaging material.

Enhancing Accessibility and Inclusivity

AI is breaking down barriers to education, making learning more accessible and inclusive for diverse populations, including those with disabilities or language differences.

- **Real-time Translation and Transcription:** AI-powered tools can translate lectures and educational materials in real-time, making content accessible to students who speak different languages. Similarly, speech-to-text and text-to-speech technologies assist students with hearing or visual impairments.
- **Adaptive Interfaces:** AI can customize user interfaces of learning platforms to accommodate various cognitive and physical needs, ensuring that students with disabilities can interact effectively with educational content.
- **Early Identification of Learning Difficulties:** AI can analyze student performance data to identify early signs of learning difficulties or disengagement, allowing educators to manually intervene proactively with targeted support.

Automating Administrative and Assessment Tasks

AI can significantly reduce the administrative burden on educators, freeing up their time to focus on teaching, mentoring, and fostering deeper student relationships.

- **Automated Grading and Feedback:** AI can grade various assignments, from multiple-choice quizzes to essays and coding exercises, providing instant, objective feedback to students. This allows students to learn from their mistakes immediately and teachers to focus on qualitative feedback.

- **Curriculum Development and Resource Management:** AI can assist educators in designing syllabuses by analyzing learning objectives, identifying relevant resources, and even suggesting optimal sequencing of topics. It can also manage and organize vast libraries of educational materials.
- **Predictive Analytics for Student Success:** AI models can predict student performance and identify those at risk of falling behind, enabling timely interventions and support strategies.

Futurism in Education: Beyond the Classroom

The true transformative potential of AI in education lies in its ability to shape futurist. AI is preparing individuals for an ever-evolving world and fostering a new generation of human beings capable of navigating complex challenges.

AI based skills readiness in India and worldwide

India is the largest human resource pool for technology skills in the world and AI is quickly shaping up to be the cutting-edge technology that everyone wants to learn. In a recent initiative EY and Microsoft have planned and launched a free online program called "AI Skills Passport". This program provides equitable access to AI education for youth aged 16 and older. This program is expected to help individuals to upskill and be future ready in an increasingly digital landscape driven by AI.

This program also called "AISP" is intended to be available worldwide, and the rollout is happening for various countries as you read about it here. The Main goal is to democratize access to AI education, ensuring AI skills is built in an equitable way. Such initiatives help nations build human capital and reduce AI based skill poverty. It enables youth employment, and reduces inequalities in access to future oriented cutting-edge technology education.

Few other similar approaches are:

Use Case 1: A Global AI-Powered Learning System

Imagine a future where education is not confined to physical institutions but is a fluid, lifelong journey within a Global AI-Powered Learning Ecosystem. This ecosystem, powered by advanced AI, would be a decentralized, interconnected network of learning resources, AI tutors, and collaborative intelligence.

- **Personalized Life-Long Learning Paths:** would continuously adapt to an individual's evolving career aspirations, personal interests, and societal needs. AI would identify skill gaps, recommend relevant micro-credentials or immersive experiences, and even simulate future job roles to prepare learners for emerging industries.
- **AI-Facilitated Global Collaboration:** Students from diverse cultural backgrounds would collaborate on complex, real-world problems, guided by AI. The AI would facilitate communication, bridge language barriers, and ensure equitable participation, fostering global citizenship and problem-solving skills essential for addressing planetary challenges.

- **Immersive Learning Simulations:** AI-driven virtual and augmented reality environments would allow students to experience historical events, explore complex scientific phenomena, or practice critical skills in risk-free simulations. For example, aspiring engineers could design and test sustainable urban infrastructures in a simulated smart city, with AI providing real-time feedback on environmental impact and efficiency.

Use Case 2: Neuro-Adaptive Learning Interfaces

Pushing the boundaries of personalization, future AI in education could integrate with neuro-adaptive interfaces, directly responding to a learner's cognitive state.

- **Real-time Cognitive Load Adjustment:** AI would monitor brain activity (e.g., via non-invasive EEG "electroencephalogram" sensors) to detect signs of cognitive overload or disengagement. It would then dynamically adjust the complexity of the material, the pace of instruction, or introduce breaks to optimize learning efficiency and prevent burnout.
- **Personalized Neuro-Feedback for Skill Acquisition:** For complex skills like advanced electromagnetics, surgery, or musical performance, AI could provide real-time neuro-feedback, guiding learners to achieve optimal brain states for focus, creativity, or motor control. This would accelerate skill acquisition and mastery.

Use Case 3: Ethical AI for Wisdom and Critical Thinking

Beyond knowledge acquisition, AI will be crucial in cultivating wisdom, critical thinking, and ethical reasoning in future generations.

- **AI-Driven Socratic Dialogues:** AI would engage students in sophisticated Socratic dialogues, challenging assumptions, prompting deeper inquiry, and exposing logical fallacies. This would hone critical thinking skills and the ability to evaluate complex information from multiple perspectives.
- **Ethical Dilemma Simulators:** AI would present students with realistic ethical dilemmas (e.g., in AI development, resource allocation, or social policy) and guide them through the process of ethical reasoning, considering various stakeholders and potential consequences. This would foster moral imagination and responsible decision-making.
- **Bias Detection and Mitigation Training:** AI would train students to identify and mitigate biases in data, algorithms, and human reasoning, preparing them to be responsible creators and consumers of AI technologies.

Challenges and Ethical Considerations

The integration of AI into education, while promising, also presents significant challenges and ethical considerations that must be proactively addressed:

- **Human Element in Education:** Over-reliance on AI could diminish the invaluable role of human educators in fostering social-emotional development, critical thinking, and mentorship. AI should augment, not replace, human interaction.

- **Data Privacy and Security:** The collection of vast amounts of student data for personalization raises concerns about privacy, data security, and potential misuse. Robust safeguards and transparent policies are essential.
- **Algorithmic Bias:** AI systems trained on biased data could perpetuate or even amplify educational inequalities, leading to discriminatory outcomes for certain student demographics. Continuous auditing and mitigation of bias are crucial.
- **Digital Divide:** Unequal access to technology and high-speed internet could exacerbate existing educational disparities, creating a new form of digital divide.
- **Ethical AI Literacy:** It is imperative to educate students and educators alike on the ethical implications of AI, fostering critical AI literacy to ensure responsible development and use.
- **Job Transformation for Educators:** The role of educators will evolve, requiring new skills in leveraging AI tools, designing AI-augmented syllabuses, and focusing on higher-order thinking and socio-emotional development.

Conclusion

Artificial Intelligence holds the key to unlocking a truly personalized and transformative educational experience for future generations. By adapting to individual needs, enhancing accessibility, automating routine tasks, and enabling futurist learning environments, AI can empower every student to reach their full potential. The journey towards this AI-augmented educational future requires careful navigation of ethical challenges, ensuring that technology serves humanity's highest aspirations. By embracing AI responsibly, we can cultivate a generation of intelligent, adaptable, and ethically conscious individuals, equipped to thrive in a world increasingly shaped by artificial intelligence, and capable of guiding humanity's ongoing transformation. The synergy between human educators and advanced AI systems promises a future where learning is more engaging, effective, and accessible for everyone, fostering a generation equipped to tackle the complex challenges of tomorrow.

FINAL TAKE: A WORLD RESHAPED BY AI

We stand at the frontier of a transformation that rivals the industrial revolution in magnitude and reach. ***AI Today and Its Evolution*** is more than a chronicle of emerging technologies, it's a lens into how intelligence, once uniquely human, is now being extended, amplified, and scaled by machines.

From its philosophical beginnings to machine learning breakthroughs, from neural networks to explainable AI, and from humanoid robots to decentralized intelligence, AI has grown into a force that is reshaping how we learn, work, heal, govern, and imagine the future. Across education, healthcare, finance, sustainability, and more, AI is not just automating tasks, it is augmenting human potential.

However, this journey is not without its challenges. Ethical dilemmas, data governance, regulatory debates, and workforce shifts underscore the importance of balancing innovation with responsibility. Throughout this book, I've emphasized that the most profound AI systems are not those that replace us, but those that help us become better versions of ourselves.

Our role is to shape AI, not as a distant force, but as an inclusive companion in humanity's next chapter. We are the stewards of this intelligence. Our choices, what we build, protect, share, and question, will define the trajectory of AI and its impact on generations to come.

The future of AI is not a mystery waiting to be unveiled. It is a reality we are actively designing. In that design lies our greatest responsibility and our greatest opportunity.

For further inquires please contact at this
email ID: aitodayandevolution@gmail.com

Glossary

A

- **AI (Artificial Intelligence):** The ability of a machine or computer system to perform tasks that typically require human intelligence.
- **AGI (Artificial General Intelligence):** A theoretical concept where AI possesses the ability to understand, learn, and apply intelligence to any intellectual task that a human being can.
- **ANI (Artificial Narrow Intelligence):** Also known as Weak AI, this is the only type of AI that currently exists, designed and trained for a specific task.
- **ASI (Artificial Superintelligence):** A theoretical concept representing an AI that would not only match but surpass human intelligence in virtually every field.
- **Algorithmic Bias:** Bias introduced during AI model design or training, often reflecting societal prejudices in data.
- **Agentic AI:** AI systems designed to act autonomously to achieve specific goals, often by breaking down complex tasks into smaller sub-tasks, executing them, and reflecting on the results.

B

- **Blockchain:** A decentralized, immutable, and transparent distributed ledger technology that records transactions across a network.

C

- **Computer Vision (CV):** An AI field that trains computers to "see" and interpret the visual world, enabling machines to process, analyze, and understand images and videos.
- **Conversational AI:** Enables machines to understand, process, and respond to human language in a natural and intuitive way.

D

- **Deep Learning (DL):** A subfield of machine learning that uses artificial neural networks with multiple layers to learn from vast amounts of data.
- **Diffusion Models:** A class of generative models that have led to impressive text-to-image generation capabilities.

E

- **Expert Systems:** Early forms of AI that use a knowledge base of human expertise to solve problems that typically require human intelligence.
- **Explainable AI (XAI):** A concept aiming to make complex AI models more transparent and understandable to humans.

G

- **Generative AI:** AI systems capable of creating new, original content, such as text, images, audio, video, and even code, that resembles human-created output.
- **GPU (Graphics Processing Unit):** A specialized electronic circuit designed to rapidly manipulate and alter memory to accelerate the creation of images in a frame buffer intended for

output to a display device. Highly effective for parallel computations required by neural networks.

L

- **Limited Memory AI:** AI systems that can look into the past to make decisions, storing and using past data for a short period to make predictions or take actions.
- **LLM (Large Language Model):** Highly powerful language models, often built upon the Transformer architecture, capable of generating human-like text.

M

- **Machine Learning (ML):** A core subset of AI that focuses on algorithms enabling systems to learn from data without explicit programming.

N

- **Natural Language Processing (NLP):** An AI field focused on enabling computers to understand, interpret, and generate human language.
- **NLU/NLG (Natural Language Understanding/Generation):** The ability to comprehend, interpret, and generate human language in both written and spoken forms.

P

- **Predictive AI:** Focuses on forecasting future outcomes or behaviors based on historical data and statistical models.

R

- **Reactive Machines:** The most basic type of AI, with no memory, reacting to current situations based on their programming.
- **Reinforcement Learning:** A type of machine learning where an agent learns to make decisions by performing actions in an environment to maximize a cumulative reward.
- **Robotics:** An interdisciplinary field that integrates AI with engineering to design, build, operate, and apply robots.

S

- **Smart Contracts:** Self-executing contracts with the terms of the agreement directly written into code, automating processes and ensuring compliance.

T

- **Turing Test:** A test proposed by Alan Turing to determine if a machine can exhibit intelligent behavior equivalent to, or indistinguishable from, that of a human.
- **Transformer Architecture:** A neural network architecture that revolutionized natural language processing, enabling models to process long sequences of text more efficiently and effectively.
- **Theory of Mind AI:** A theoretical concept referring to AI systems capable of understanding emotions, beliefs, intentions, and desires of other intelligent entities.

V

- **Vibe Coding:** An approach where developers heavily rely on large language models (LLMs) to generate code.

- **Vibe Flows:** The state of continuous, intuitive, and highly productive workflow enabled by AI integration in software development.
- **Vibestack:** The collection of AI-powered tools and platforms that facilitate vibe coding and enable enhanced development workflows.

REFERENCES

This reference section provides a comprehensive list of sources consulted during the research and writing of "AI Today and Its Evolution." All sources are publicly available and have been selected to ensure compliance with copyright requirements for worldwide publication. Thank you to each and every one of them for sharing the knowledge.

https://www.ibm.com/think/topics/artificial-intelligence-types

https://www.mckinsey.com/capabilities/mckinsey-digital/our-insights/the-economic-potential-of-generative-ai-the-next-productivity-frontier

https://www.techtarget.com/searchenterpriseai/feature/Attributes-of-open-vs-closed-AI-explained

https://www.multimodal.dev/post/open-source-ai-vs-closed-source-ai

https://bipartisanpolicy.org/blog/the-open-or-closed-ai-dilemma/

https://www.theartnewspaper.com/2024/05/22/the-difference-between-open-ai-and-closed-aiand-why-it-matters

https://formtek.com/blog/open-ai-vs-closed-ai-whats-the-difference-and-why-does-it-matter/

https://www.forbes.com/sites/bernardmarr/2024/04/22/navigating-the-generative-ai-divide-open-source-vs-closed-source-solutions/

https://www.sharp.co.uk/news-and-events/blog/the-differences-between-closed-and-open-ai

https://medium.com/@rsudha222/open-vs-closed-ai-models-the-eternal-tug-of-war-5881a7159590

https://www.sonatype.com/blog/beyond-open-vs.-closed-understanding-the-spectrum-of-ai-transparency

https://www.copyright.gov/ai/

https://www.congress.gov/crs-product/LSB10922

https://www.rand.org/pubs/perspectives/PEA3243-1.html

https://www.wipo.int/web/wipo-magazine/articles/us-copyright-office-on-ai-human-creativity-still-matters-legally-73696

https://nysba.org/copyright-law-in-the-age-of-ai-navigating-authorship-infringement-and-creative-rights/?srsltid=AfmBOopSwwTXorCX2pVzhGDRbaoVhxwmY1kMVvVwnsYgibDgiHik86BT

https://www.whitecase.com/insight-our-thinking/ai-watch-global-regulatory-tracker-united-states

https://www.copyright.gov/newsnet/2025/1060.html

https://www.brookings.edu/articles/ai-and-the-visual-arts-the-case-for-copyright-protection/

https://www.jdsupra.com/legalnews/us-copyright-office-releases-third-8205239/

https://www.bclplaw.com/en-US/events-insights-news/us-state-by-state-artificial-intelligence-legislation-snapshot.html

https://europrospects.eu/the-eu-ai-acts-copyright-loophole-a-threat-to-creative-rights/

https://www.morganlewis.com/pubs/2024/02/eu-ai-act-how-far-will-eu-copyright-principles-extend

https://www.theguardian.com/technology/2025/feb/19/eu-accused-of-leaving-devastating-copyright-loophole-in-ai-act

https://www.europarl.europa.eu/topics/en/article/20230601STO93804/eu-ai-act-first-regulation-on-artificial-intelligence

https://www.bruegel.org/newsletter/why-should-eu-copyright-protection-be-reduced-realise-innovation-benefits-generative-ai

https://www.isaca.org/resources/white-papers/2024/understanding-the-eu-ai-act

https://onlinelibrary.wiley.com/doi/10.1111/jwip.12330

https://medium.com/@adnanmasood/ais-regulatory-reckoning-eu-ai-act-and-ripple-effects-on-u-s-technology-policy-c03c30d6a6a0

https://law.asia/russia-ai-regulations-legal-framework-ethics/

https://www.cna.org/our-media/newsletters/ai-and-autonomy-in-russia

https://globalailaw.com/russia-ai-law/

https://thebulletin.org/2025/03/russian-networks-flood-the-internet-with-propaganda-aiming-to-corrupt-ai-chatbots/

https://www.lexology.com/library/detail.aspx?g=74480340-bf4a-4f5d-bc77-54d65dd4c26d

https://freedomhouse.org/country/russia/freedom-net/2024

https://www.researchgate.net/publication/347918108_Russian_experience_of_using_digital_technologies_and_legal_risks_of_AI

https://www.techpolicy.press/ai-training-and-copyright-infringement-solutions-from-asia/

https://www.privacyworld.blog/2024/03/japans-new-draft-guidelines-on-ai-and-copyright-is-it-really-ok-to-train-ai-using-pirated-materials/

https://datamatters.sidley.com/2024/08/16/asia-pacific-regulations-keep-pace-with-rapid-evolution-of-artificial-intelligence-technology/

https://cepa.org/article/ai-boom-or-copyright-doom-lessons-from-asia/

https://www.elastic.co/blog/artificial-intelligence-regulation-asia-comparative-analysis

https://www.semafor.com/article/12/04/2023/china-ai-copyright-court-ruling

https://natlawreview.com/article/artificial-intelligence-and-intellectual-property-legal-frameworks-asia-pacific

https://bowergroupasia.com/ai-regulations-global-trends-challenges-and-approaches/

https://www.lexology.com/library/detail.aspx?g=42711d52-4d44-4d8d-a8c8-683111df8d2b

https://www.techinasia.com/question/how-will-ai-copyright-rulings-affect-tech-startups-in-asia

https://www.ey.com/en_gl/ai-skills-passport

https://www.ey.com/en_in/newsroom/2025/10/ey-and-microsoft-launch-ai-skills-passport-to-equip-india-s-youth-with-ai-driven-future

Open-Source and Royalty-Free Sources

Linux Foundation. "Hyperledger Fabric Documentation." *Hyperledger Project.*

Google. "TensorFlow: Open Source Machine Learning Library."

Ocean Protocol. "AI and Blockchain Use Cases for Data Marketplaces."

Fetch.ai. "AI Agent Documentation."

arXiv.org. Open-Access Scientific Papers on AI/Blockchain Convergence.

Organisation for Economic Co-operation and Development (OECD). AI Policy Observatory

Stanford University. AI Index 2023: Trends and Analytics in AI Development

IBM Corporation. Blockchain Platform Documentation

World Economic Forum. Reports on AI in Financial Services

Salesforce. Articles on AI in Banking.

IMD Business School. Articles on AI in Financial Services.

eMarketer. Guides on AI in Finance

Congressional Research Service. Reports on AI and Machine Learning in Financial Services.

DigitalDefynd. Case Studies on AI in Banking

Vonage. Articles on AI in Banking

McKinsey & Company. Reports on Building the AI Bank of the Future

GlobeNewswire. Press Releases on Generative AI in Banking and Finance

RareConnections. Real-World Examples of AI in Banking

Built In. Real-World Examples of AI in Banking.

NatWest Group. Insights on Harnessing AI in Banking
Enxoo. "Articles on AI in Financial Services.
Google Cloud. Resources on AI in Finance
CIOCoverage. Real-World Examples of AI in Finance
HiverHQ. Real-World Examples of AI in Finance
Smarttek Solutions. AI Use Cases in Insurance
TestingXperts. Generative AI and Document Automation in Insurance
Multimodal.dev. Generative AI and Document Automation in Insurance
Bridgenext. Insights on Insurance Automation
Fintech Global. Insights on Insurance Automation
Foliume. Overviews of AI in Insurance
KPMG. Overviews of AI in Insurance
The Zebra. Future Outlook of AI in Insurance
McKinsey & Company. Future Outlook of AI in Insurance
Salesforce. Real-World Examples of AI in Insurance
Multimodal.dev. AI-Powered Automation for Credit Unions
CUInsight. AI in Credit Unions and Digital Transformation
Interface.ai. AI Agents for Credit Unions
Alkami. How AI Helps Credit Unions Compete
Forbes. How AI Helps Credit Unions Compete
Inclind, Inc. AI Use Cases and Examples in Credit Unions
CreditUnions.com. AI Use Cases and Examples in Credit Unions
Symphonize. AI Use Cases and Examples in Credit Unions
Risk.net. AI in Capital Markets Automation and Predictive Precision
International Monetary Fund (IMF). Articles on AI's Impact on Financial Markets

Commodity Futures Trading Commission (CFTC). Reports on AI in Financial Markets

Broadridge. Intelligent Automation in Capital Markets

The Wall Street Journal. How AI is Transforming Banking and Capital Markets

Deloitte. How AI is Transforming Banking and Capital Markets

Capital Group. Future Outlook of AI in Capital Markets

London Stock Exchange Group (LSEG). Future Outlook of AI in Capital Markets

Datos Insights. AI Use Cases and Examples in Capital Markets

International Organization of Securities Commissions (IOSCO). AI Use Cases and Examples in Capital Markets

Kx Systems. AI Use Cases and Examples in Capital Markets

Softkraft.co. General AI Use Cases in Real Estate

Multifamily Dive. AI Applications in Multi-Family Real Estate

Forbes. Insights into AI's Impact on Multifamily Investing

Adventures in CRE. AI Tools in Commercial Real Estate

CBIZ. How AI is Transforming Commercial Real Estate

JLL (Jones Lang LaSalle). AI's Impact on Hotels and Hospitality

Plotzy.ai. AI in Mixed-Use Real Estate Strategies

Inside Self Storage. AI in Self-Storage Facilities

Tolj Commercial. Automated Warehouses in Industrial Real Estate

Deloitte. AI's Impact on Data Centers

Entrepreneur. AI's Influence on Real Estate Development

Landgate. AI in Undeveloped Land and Listing Descriptions

Strutt & Parker. AI's Role in Agricultural Real Estate.

AcreTrader. AI in Farmland Investing

Shutterstock. Royalty-Free Images and General Concepts Related to AI and Environmental Protection

Freepik. Royalty-Free Images and General Concepts Related to AI and Environmental Protection

Wildlife.AI. Educational Programs and News on AI in Conservation

The Conservation Foundation. Insights on AI's Role in Conservation Efforts

California Council on Science and Technology (CCST). AI Tools for Addressing Conservation and Biodiversity

Appsilon. Information on Mbaza AI for Biodiversity Monitoring

AI for Good (International Telecommunication Union). How AI Technologies Provide Valuable Insights into Biodiversity Changes

Phys.org. Studies on AI's Potential to Advance Biodiversity Conservation

Center for Mathematical Research (CMR), UC Berkeley. How AI Systems Can Help Companies Preserve Biodiversity.

Nordeco.dk. Ideas on How AI Could Revolutionize Biodiversity Conservation

Nature. Articles on Improving Biodiversity Protection Through Artificial Intelligence

Yale Environment 360. Features on How AI is Transforming Conservation Science

Microsoft. Announcements on AI Tools like SPARROW for Biodiversity Protection

IBM. Articles on AI's Role in Protecting Biodiversity.

Freepik. Royalty-Free Images Related to AI Climate Change Mitigation

Climate Change AI. Work at the Intersection of Climate Change and Machine Learning

Global Partnership on Artificial Intelligence (GPAI). PDF Reports on Climate Change and AI.

World Journal of Advanced Research and Reviews (WJARR). Papers Reviewing the Role of AI in Climate Change Mitigation

Innovation for Cool Earth Forum (ICEF). Roadmaps on AI for Climate Change Mitigation

Scientific Research Publishing (SCIRP). Studies on the Socio-Technical Framework for Evaluating AI's Effectiveness in Climate Change Mitigation

Center on Global Energy Policy, Columbia University. Insights on AI for Climate Change Mitigation

Nature. Articles on the Role of AI in the Climate Transition

ResearchGate. Academic Publications on AI for Climate Change Mitigation

All sources referenced in this book have been carefully selected to ensure compliance with copyright requirements for worldwide publication. The sources fall into the following categories:

- **Open-access academic publications** with Creative Commons or similar open licenses
- **Government and institutional publications** in the public domain
- **Corporate documentation and reports** made freely available for educational and research purposes
- **News articles and blog posts** from reputable sources used under fair use provisions for educational and informational purposes
- **Open-source software documentation** with permissive licenses (Apache 2.0, MIT, etc.)

The content derived from these sources has been synthesized, analyzed, and presented in a format that adds significant scholarly value while respecting the intellectual property rights of the original authors and publishers.

For readers interested in exploring these topics further, encourage direct consultation of the original sources listed above, as they provide valuable detailed information and ongoing updates in the rapidly evolving field of artificial intelligence.